ANDERSONVILLE
GEORGIA
U★S★A

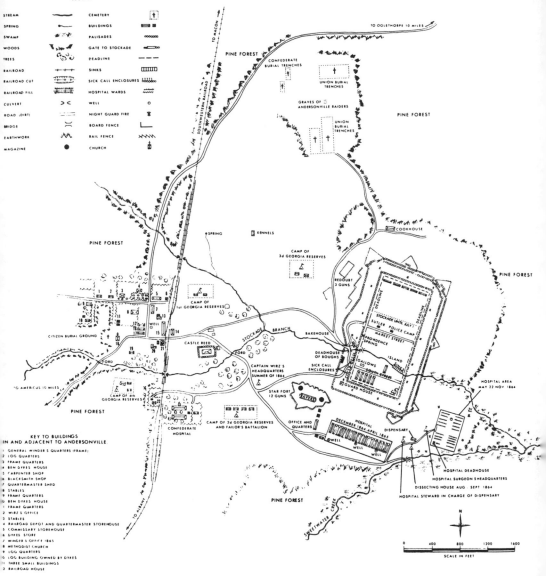

ANDERSONVILLE NATIONAL HISTORIC SITE
GEORGIA

HISTORICAL BASE MAP
1864—1865

UNITED STATES DEPARTMENT OF THE INTERIOR
NATIONAL PARK SERVICE

ANDERSONVILLE
GEORGIA
U*S*A

by

Peggy Sheppard

Sheppard Publications

Andersonville, Georgia 31711

Acknowledgments

I am deeply indebted to Mrs. Ann E. Lewis, founder and long-time editor of *Georgia Magazine,* whose help and guidance made possible this publication. Special thanks also go to Gammage Shivers, Modern Studios, Americus, Georgia, Mrs. Alfred Schild, Dean of Women, Georgia Southwestern College, and to Mrs. Louie Brightwell and the entire staff of the Lake Blackshear Regional Library, Americus.

Cover design by John Kollock

Contents

1 ANDERSONVILLE, THE MUCH TOLD TALE.......... 9

2 HENRY WIRZ — MONSTER OR MARTYR?.......... 15

3 THE CLERGY AND ANDERSONVILLE PRISON....... 33

4 ANDERSONVILLE HONEYMOON................... 38

5 THE PRISON AND THE NEIGHBORHOOD........... 40

6 CLARA BARTON AT ANDERSONVILLE............. 45

7 THE TRIALS OF THE WIRZ MONUMENT........... 58

8 THE FREEDMAN'S SCHOOL...................... 66

9 THE HODGES PLANTATION...................... 69

10 ANDERSONVILLE MINING ACTIVITIES............. 79

11 THE MYSTERY OF ANDERSONVILLE METHODIST
   CHURCH 83

12 JIMMY LAWRENCE AND PENNINGTON SAINT
   JAMES CHURCH................................... 87

   BIBLIOGRAPHY 93

   ABOUT THE AUTHOR 94

Artist's conception of Andersonville Stockade as it looked at the peak of its occupancy. From an original color lithograph of a painting made in 1884.

1

Andersonville
The Much Told Tale

T HE TALE OF ANDERSONVILLE has been told many times. Surviving
prisoners left memoirs, letters, diaries, and books about their
experiences. Reams of official testimony built up during the United
States military trial of Captain Henry Wirz, keeper of the prison, for
alleged brutalities to Union soldiers confined there. The trial, conviction, and execution of Captain Wirz set off a nation-wide wave of
public feeling and controversy.

Anderson Station, as it was called at the time, was selected as a
prison site early in 1864 when Generals Lee and Grant fought in
Virginia and thousands of troops were taken prisoner by each side.
It was far from the Union lines in the cotton growing region of Georgia
near the end of the Southwestern Railroad.

The prison was hastily established in an oak and pine forest through
which ran a creek. Labor was impressed from surrounding plantations.
Tall pine trees were felled, trimmed, and hacked to 20-foot lengths.
These logs were used to build a double stockade wall about fifteen feet
high. The inner wall stretched 750 by 1,540 feet and embraced 26½
acres. Sentry boxes were placed at intervals along the top of the inner
stockade. A deadline, twenty feet inside the inner stockade walls,
marked by slat-topped poles driven into the ground, further restricted
the inhabitable area of the prison enclosure.

As the first Union soldiers arrived on February 25, 1864, they
found no housing and no sanitary facilities, but simply this huge corral
in which they were penned. Haphazardly they built "shebangs" —
shelters of any material they could find. These included huts and
lean-tos from logs, limbs, bushes, clay, and brush left within the prison
walls. Blankets, tent flies, and overcoats were also used in building
shelters. Lacking materials, some prisoners dug holes in the side of
a hill for shelter.

The creek, which provided the prisoners' drinking water, also
absorbed their sewage. Adding to the pollution of the creek, were the
latrines of the Confederate guards who were housed upstream from
the stockade. Offal from the camp bakery, near the guards' quarters,
was dumped into the stream. It was inevitable that scurvy, diarrhea,

gangrenous sores, dysentery, and other sicknesses should break out in epidemic proportion.

Although the prison was originally planned for 6,000 men, prisoners poured into the stockade throughout the spring and summer of 1864 until there were over three times that number. The poverty of the Confederacy, a defective transportation system, and the Union blockade of needed supplies, prevented the prison officials from building barracks, and supplying cooked food, clothing, or adequate medical care for their charges. Innummerable deaths and indescribable suffering resulted.

Adding to the prisoners' troubles were the "Raiders," a gang of 500 thugs, most of whom were from the slums of New York City. They beat and murdered their fellow prisoners in order to steal from them food, clothing, and other necessities of life. The lawlessness of the Raiders led to such loud prisoner complaints that Confederate authorities seized some of the worst Raider offenders. The prisoners were authorized to try the accused robbers and muderers. The prisoners' court session lasted several weeks. Some of the offenders were severely beaten when forced to run between lines of prisoners armed with sticks and other weapons. Six Raiders were sentenced to death and hanged from a scaffold inside the prison. The graves of the executed six are located a discreet distance from the 12,912 graves of other prison casualties at Andersonville.

Descendants of Union soldiers have long associated the name of Captain Wirz, his superior officer, General John H. Winder, and the South generally, with the high mortality and the stories of hunger, thirst, exposure, filth, and disease endured by the 45,613 prisoners of war confined at Andersonville during its 14 months of operation.

Defenders of the Confederacy point out that mortality was high among the Confederate guards as well as Union prisoners and that the Federals declared medicine contraband and refused to permit supplies to go to the prison. In August 1864, when the death rate at Andersonville was highest, the Confederates offered to deliver all sick and wounded to the Federals without requiring an equivalent of their own men in return, but the offer was not accepted until December, after most of the deaths had occurred. Today the opinion of many Civil War students is that Captain Wirz probably did the best he could with what the destitute Confederacy could provide him.

His defenders say that Captain Wirz was made the scapegoat and alone took all the blame for conditions at the prison. His superior officer, General Winder, died of a heart attack before the end of the war.

Scene inside stockade, Andersonville Prison. Reproduced from the collection of the National Archives.

11

Evidence came to light later that Wirz was offered a pardon on condition he would implicate President of the Confederacy Jefferson Davis in a Confederate plot to kill great numbers of Union prisoners by starvation and exposure to the elements, but that he rejected the offer.

In 1909, forty-four years after the Wirz execution, outraged members of the Georgia Division of the United Daughters of the Confederacy erected a tall shaft in the center of the village of Andersonville in memory of Captain Wirz. Its purpose, says the inscription, is "to rescue his name from the stigma attached to it by embittered prejudice. He indignantly spurned a pardon proffered on condition he would incriminate President Davis and thus exonerate himself from charges of which both were innocent." The monument stands today, dust covered, in the center of the sleepy little town of some 300 citizens.

In 1956, ninety-one years after Wirz's execution, Thomas Spencer, an Atlanta writer, Civil War student, and strong defender of Captain Wirz, at his own expense, purchased a marble headstone for the grave of Captain Wirz in Washington, D. C. The United Daughters of the Confederacy paid for installing the monument in Mt. Olivet Cemetery. The inscription reads: "Captain Henry Wirz, C. S. A. Confederate Hero - Martyr. Died Nov. 10, 1865."

In the beauty and serenity of the present day prison park it is difficult for visitors to visualize the scene more than one hundred years ago when a wretched crowd of 33,000 sick, starving, dirty human beings existed in filth and squalor in thousands of huts, lean-tos, and dugouts, all massed together within a stockaded area of 26 acres. Today, on the lush, immaculate, green grounds, visitors can view the outline of the famous stockade of Camp Sumter where up to 45,000 Union soldiers were imprisoned. They can see 27 deep wells dug by prisoners with their bare hands or with improvised tools in their frantic search for fresh drinking water when Stockade Creek, which still flows through the grounds, became polluted. Tunnels, which the prisoners fashioned for escape purposes and where many perished in cave-ins, can be viewed today. Providence Spring, which legend says gushed forth in answer to the prayers of the prisoners dying of thirst, is still bubbling pure water. Natives of the area say that the spring had been there years before the War, that it had been a favorite deer stand for local hunters and that when the breastworks for Camp Sumter were hastily thrown up, dirt and debris covered the watering place and closed the spring. In August 1864, a thunderstorm moved the debris, thus providentially opening the old spring and providing fresh water for the prisoners.

12

In Andersonville National Cemetery, headstones mark the final resting place of 12,912 Union soldiers who died there between February 1864 and April 1865. Most stones bear the name, home state, and monument number of the man buried there. On more than 500 stones there is only one word, "Unknown."

Towering high above the individual tombstones are larger statuary dedicated by various states to their own dead. Most of these monuments have been erected since 1900. New Jersey took the lead in 1899 by erecting a $2000 monument to her 235 sons who died at Andersonville. Massachusetts, with 767 known dead; Maine, with 252; Pennsylvania, 1,849 known dead; Iowa 214; Indiana, 702; Rhode Island, 79; New York, 2,261; Wisconsin, 378; Connecticut, 290; Illinois 850; Tennessee, 1284; Ohio 1055; Michigan, 638; and Minnesota, 79 known dead, followed suit, so that in the next 15 years, Andersonville was visited by 15 delegations from Northern states, often including the governor or lieutenant governor and other high-ranking state officials, for the dedication of these monuments.

Clara Barton, famed Civil War nurse, had laid the groundwork for these state monuments by coming to Andersonville with a Federal expedition of 34 workmen on July 25, 1865, just 4 months after the war ended, for the purpose of identifying the graves and enclosing the grounds of the cemetery.

In the five years after the Civil War, the bodies of 347 other Union casualties who had died in Georgia (most of them were with Sherman's army as it marched through Georgia) were moved to Andersonville National Cemetery. Approximately one thousand United States Armed Forces veterans (Spanish American War veterans, World War I and II veterans, veterans of the Korean and Vietnam conflicts) now sleep with the Civil War dead. A few women and children, dependents of veterans, are also buried there. Color guards from Fort Benning and other Georgia military bases often furnish military burial honors.

At Clara Barton's suggestion, the land comprising the prison as well as the cemetery was appropriated by the United States government. Ben Dykes and Elizabeth Dykes, former owners of the land received $3300 from the United States government for 120 acres on February 9, 1875. In 1879, the tract containing the prison and fortifications became the property of the Women's Relief Corps Auxiliary of the Grand Army of the Republic which purchased an additional 14½ acres and undertook the beautification and care of the prison and fortification sites. In 1910, this organization donated the property now known as Andersonville Prison Park to the United States government.

A few landmarks of the past remain in the area. Not far from the Wirz monument in the center of the town of Andersonville, is the present home of the W. L. Easterlin family, which is said to be the house where Gen. Winder lived during his command of the prison. One of Mr. Easterlin's ancestors, J. J. Easterlin, was on the staff of the stockade commander at the time of the surrender of the fort. The frame building, now housing the Andersonville post office, is said to have been a tavern at the time of the War. Southwest of the town in Freedman's Hill where a mission school, established by the Congregational Society of Barrington, Rhode Island, for the offspring of freed slaves, flourished from 1866 until 1920.

Another landmark of the past is the beautiful ante-bellum plantation home of Mrs. R. J. Hodges, overlooking part of Sweetwater Creek about two miles south of the Prison Park. This imposing two-story structure was built with slave labor by Judge Robert James Hodges in 1842. The general construction of the house has been preserved much as it was in those days.

Shack used by Captain Wirz as office 1864-1865.

14

2

Henry Wirz –
Monster or Martyr?

O N AUGUST 23, 1865, less than five months after the surrender of
Lee at Appomattox, Captain Henry Wirz, keeper of Andersonville
Prison, was brought to trial in Washington, D.C. before a special
military commission by order of the President of the United States.
The commission tried Wirz on two charges. The first was that "he
maliciously, willfully, and traitorously . . . conspired with John H.
Winder, Richard B. Winder, W. S. Winder, Joseph White, R. R. Stevenson, and others unknown, to impair and injure the health and destroy
the lives of soldiers of war within the lines of the so-called Confederate
States in the military prisons thereof, to the end that the armies of
the United States might be weakened and impaired; in violation of the
laws and customs of war . . ." In the second charge, he was tried for
thirteen murders of individual prisoners listed thus: that he personally
shot three unknown prisoners to death with a revolver, that he stamped
one unknown prisoner to death, that he confined two unknown prisoners in stocks which confinement led to their deaths, that he had bound
the neck and feet of one unknown prisoner with chains and iron balls
which led to that prisoner's death, that he ordered a sentinel to shoot
and kill four unknown prisoners, that he personally beat an unknown
prisoner on the head with a revolver which caused the prisoner's death,
that he set ferocious dogs in pursuit of an unknown prisoner which
led to the prisoner's death.

The court found Wirz guilty of the first charge. In considering the
second charge, the court found the prisoner guilty of eleven distinct
murders out of the thirteen charged, and of three murders by use of
dogs, not charged, but shown by the evidence. He was sentenced to
death by hanging and was so executed in Washington, D. C. on
November 10, 1865.

Henry Wirz, a native of Switzerland, who had come to this country
in 1849 at the age of 31, was living in Louisiana when the Civil War
broke out and he decided to join the Confederacy. He enlisted in the
Fourth Louisiana Infantry on June 16, 1861 and became a sergeant
by the spring of 1862 when he was wounded just above the right wrist
during the Battle of Seven Pines. This injury was a source of physical

15

Captain Henry Wirz (from Confederate Veteran Magazine, 1864)

discomfort for the rest of his life. He was promoted to captain on June 12, 1862 and was detailed as acting Adjutant General to Gen John H. Winder who assigned him to command the military prison at Richmond, Virginia in late August. He stayed one month at Richmond and then was sent on a mission to Alabama in search of missing records. He was then given command of the prison at Tuscaloosa, Alabama. In the latter part of 1863 he was sent by President Jefferson Davis to Europe to carry secret dispatches to the Confederate Commissioners — Mr. Mason in England and Mr. Slidell in France — and to all the financial agents of the Confederate Government in Europe. In March 1864 he was ordered to Andersonville where he was assigned keeper of the inner prison by Lt. Col. Alexander W. Persons, then commander of Andersonville Prison. He served in that capacity at Andersonville until the prison was closed on April 10, 1865, serving first under Persons and then under Gen. John H. Winder, who replaced Persons on June 17, 1864.

Even before the war ended, the Northern press had started publishing sensational stories on the horrors of Andersonville. When Henry Wirz was brought to trial, the newspapers pictured him as a brute who took delight in torturing Union prisoners. In the press, he was called, "The Fiend of Andersonville" or "The Monster of Andersonville." Public feeling was so strong against Wirz that, although he was a native of Switzerland, the Swiss Consul General in Washington refused to do anything to help him and even refused to hold in trust money which had been sent by those wishing to contribute to the financial cost of Wirz's defense. A prominent law firm of Washington, D. C., the firm of Hughes, Denver, and Peck, which at first agreed to undertake the defense of Wirz, withdrew from the case, presumably because to defend Wirz would damage the firm's reputation. Louis Schade and O. S. Baker then undertook his defense.

The trial covered a period of nearly two months, and the testimony of the witnesses, some hundred and forty in number, including the witnesses called in his behalf, covered some five thousand pages of written matter. Witness after witness, Rebel officers as well as Union prisoners, testified to the fact that the prison was woefully over-crowded. Built to contain 10,000 men, and later enlarged to accommodate 5,000 more, during most of the time more than twice that number were crowded inside the 26-acre corral. Testimony corroborated the fact that there was no shelter from the elements except such as the prisoners constructed themselves out of scrap lumber, pine boughs, clay, tenting, or clothing. All trees had been cut down inside the enclosure which resulted in the fact that no shade was available in the hundred degree heat of summer. Prisoners were without proper clothing or blankets to ward off the winter cold. Prisoners testified as to the scarcity of food, the poor quality of the food and the fact that until a cookhouse was built, all food was issued uncooked and prisoners were expected to cook their own meals, but very few utensils were available for this purpose. Testimony brought out the fact that when a cookhouse was finally built, it was located upstream outside the stockade and that garbage, grease, and offal were cast into the stream which wound through the stockade, thus polluting the stream which was intended to supply prisoners with drinking water. Testimony also brought out that open sinks set aside as privies became so clogged with human wastes that the stench was carried by prevailing winds for a distance of almost two miles and that myriads of flies abounded over the sinks.

A report received by Confederate officials at Richmond, the Confederate capital, August 17, 1864 from Colonel D. T. Chandler, Confederate Assistant Adjutant and Inspector-General, was introduced as evidence in the trial. Colonel Chandler's report describes the crowded conditions at Andersonville. His report states, "I am decidedly of opinion that not over 15,000 prisoners should be kept at this point, the running water not being sufficient for more than that number, and because it is impossible for one man to exercise a proper supervision over them, and that all over that number should be sent elsewhere. At my request a survey of the grounds has been made by Colonel Harkie, Fifty-fifth Georgia Regiment, and civil engineer, with a view to drainage. His report is herewith submitted. The necessity for it is urgent. I also recommend that a supply of clothing be furnished for issue to the prisoners and that soap and anti-scorbutics be issued to them . . . After inquiring, I am confident that by slight exertion green corn and other anti-scorbutics could readily be obtained."

Chandler's report then goes on to say that the cookhouse which had been polluting the prisoners' drinking water was in the process of being relocated and that an effort was being made by Wirz to fill up the marsh and construct a sluice — the upper end to be used for bathing, etc., and the lower end as a sink, but the difficulty to procure lumber and tools very much retarded the work, and threatened soon to stop it. His report outlines the needs of the prison hospital and then says, "In conclusion I beg leave to recommend that no more prisoners be sent to this already over-crowded prison . . . With a view of relieving to some extent this point as soon as possible, I respectfully suggest that 2,000 of those who most need the change, especially the Belle Island prisoners, be at once sent to Macon, to occupy the quarters vacated by the Federal officers, that being the greatest number that can be properly accommodated with shelter at that point."

Colonel Chandler made a supplemental report on August 5, 1864,

General John H. Winder (From the collection of the Library of Congress.)

which went forward with the principal report. In it he commends Capt. Wirz as an efficient officer and closes with the following recommendation as to General Winder:

"My duty requires me respectfully to recommend a change in the officer in command of the post, Brigadier-General J. H. Winder, and the substitution in his place of some one who unites both energy and good judgement with some feeling of humanity and consideration for the welfare and comfort (so far as is consistent with their safe-keeping) of the vast number of unfortunates placed under his control; some one who at least will not advocate deliberately and in cold blood the propriety of leaving them in their present condition until their numbers has been sufficiently reduced by death to make the present arrangement suffice for their accommodation; who will not consider it a matter of self-laudation and boasting that he has never been inside of the stockade, a place the horrors of which it is difficult to describe, and which is a disgrace to civilization; the condition of which he might, by the exercise of a little energy and judgement, even with the limited means at his command, have considerably improved."

It was brought out at the trial that no action was taken on Chandler's report, although the report was received and read by Confederate Secretary of War Seddon and other Confederate officials. Six months after making the report, Chandler went to Richmond for the purpose of trying to get some action on his report, but Seddon's resignation was pending at that time. He resigned February 7th and was succeeded by General Breckinridge. According to testimony by R.T.H. Kean, chief of the Bureau of War at Richmond, Breckinridge paid little attention to Chandler's report. It was also brought out that instead of being replaced, General Winder was promoted to Commissary-general of all Union prisoners in all Confederate prisons.

In his testimony, Dr. Joseph Jones, a surgeon of the Confederate Army, described the prison hospital as extending to within a few yards of a stream which was used as a privy and loaded with human excrement. No beds of straw were furnished hospital patients. They lay on the floor or on slabs of wood. Their wounds were washed by pouring water over them and all putrescent matter was allowed to soak into the dirt floor. He testified that, "Millions of flies swarmed over everything and covered the faces of the sleeping patients, crawled down their open mouths, and deposited maggots upon the gangrenous wounds of the living and the mouths of the dead."

Out of the 145 witnesses called, only 15 testified to any specific cruelty of Wirz toward a particular prisoner. Father Peter Whelan, the Catholic priest who had ministered to prisoners at Andersonville, testified that he never saw or heard of Wirz murdering a prisoner. Father H. Clavereul, Father Whelan's assistant, testified in the same vein. One former prisoner, Frederick Guscetti of the 47th New York Regiment not only testified in behalf of Wirz, saying that he had always been treated well by him, but also sent a letter to the editor of the *New York News* asking readers desirous of a fair trial for Wirz to send financial contributions to the Swiss Consul General in Washington and asking any former prisoners of Andersonville who would be willing to testify in behalf of Wirz to forward their names and addresses to Louis Schade, Attorney-at-law, Washington, D. C. Twelve former prisoners testified for the defense, but several witnesses against Wirz gave damning testimony to specific cruelties and murders by Wirz.

One of the witnesses against Wirz, Felix de La Baume, a prisoner, testified that he saw Wirz shoot with a revolver, two prisoners who had fallen out of ranks to go after water for another prisoner who was suffering from an epileptic fit. De La Baum testified that Wirz punished the guard who let the two men go after water, by having that guard tied up by the thumbs for two hours. He also testified that he saw a sick prisoner, an inmate of the hospital, tied with an iron collar round his neck to a post. De La Baume testified that the man was afterwards

WIRZ STAMPING ON A PRISONER

DOGS TEARING A PRISONER

HOW THEY ROBBED PRISONERS

FIGHTING FOR BONES

CRAWLING TO THE SWAMP FOR WATER

BALL & CHAIN

MUD BURROW

SHOT ON THE DEAD LINE FOR A PIECE OF MOULDY CAKE

From *Harper's Weekly*, September 16, 1865

Life in Andersonville Prison

Typical of illustrations pertaining to Andersonville which appeared in Northern publications are these from Harper's Weekly, *September* 16, 1865.

taken back to the hospital where De La Baume visited him the next day and saw his neck and tongue were so much swollen that he was unable to speak and that he died two or three days later. After the trial, evidence came to light discrediting the testimony of this witness.

George W. Gray, a prisoner, testified that he saw Wirz shoot and kill William Stewart, a private belonging to the 9th Minnesota Infantry. Gray related that he and Stewart had gone out of the stockade with a dead body. He testified, "After laying the dead body in the dead-house Captain Wirz rode up to us and asked by what authority we were out there or what we were doing there. Stewart said we were there by proper authority. Wirz said no more, but drew a revolver and shot the man. After he was killed, the guard took from the body about twenty or thirty dollars, and Wirz took the money from the guard and rode off, telling the guard to take me to prison."

Many historians feel that Henry Wirz was a scapegoat, taking all the blame and all the punishment for the conditions at Andersonville. General John H. Winder had died in February, 1865, six months befort Wirz was brought to trial, thus escaping the wrath of the Federal government which surely would have wanted to try him along with or perhaps instead of Wirz. President Johnson's military commission had at first named Jefferson Davis and Howell Cobb along with the other alleged conspirators, but those names had suddenly been dropped from the first charge against Wirz. The other alleged conspirators, Richard B. Winder, W. S. Winder, Joseph White, and R. R. Stevenson, were never brought to trial.

Some historians point out that the awful situation responsible for the indescribable sufferings and the ultimate deaths of 12,912 prisoners at Andersonville is a stain on the record of the Confederacy. On reflection, it seems to many students of history that knowing Andersonville was so over-crowded that it was impossible for the impoverished South to feed, house, or clothe the prisoners adequately enough to keep the majority of them in reasonably good health, the Confederacy should have done **something,** to alleviate the situation — even if it meant paroling the prisoners.

Confederate defenders claimed that the prisoners were fed as well as the Confederate guards, that prisoners themselves served as cooks for the prison inmates, but that the prisoners were not used to a daily diet of corn bread (often made of coarse ground corn, cobs and all) field peas, and pork fat, and that many of the prisoners were sick when they arrived at Andersonville. They point out that Confederate soldiers were in rags the same as the prisoners, that the Federals had declared medicine contraband of war and that the prison authorities had repeatedly begged to no avail for medicine for prisoners, citing the Confederacy's inability to provide adequately for those in its charge as reason for the need of exchange, but the North refused exchange. Confederate defenders point out that Jefferson Davis ordered a delegation of prisoners of Andersonville be sent to Washington to plead the cause of exchange and that such a delegation was sent, but that they were unsuccessful in their mission. Zealous Southern historians, defending the South's honor, have pointed out that the death rate in Southern prisons was nine per cent, while that in Northern prisons was twelve per cent. The figures they use are those of U. S. Secretary of War Edwin M. Stanton in a report dated July 19, 1899, in which he lists deaths in Northern prisons at 26,436 and deaths in Southern prisons at 22,756 with total Confederates in Northern prisons listed as 220,000 and total Union soldiers in Southern prisons at 270,000. General N. P. Chipman, Judge Advocate of the Military Court which tried Henry Wirz, takes some of the starch out of those statistics in his book, *The Tragedy of Andersonville,* by saying, "What they don't say is that more deaths occurred at Andersonville during the four months of June, July, August, and September of 1864 than died in the 25 prisons of the North for the entire year of 1864. There were preventable and deplorable deaths of Confederate prisoners in Northern prisons, but Northern prisons made some attempt to provide shelter to protect prisoners from the elements."

That Henry Wirz, an underling, the keeper of the inner prison under the command of first Colonel Persons and then General Winder, was not alone to blame for conditions at Andersonville seems irrefutable. That he was without money for his defense, a foreigner in his adopted country without influential relatives or friends, is also irrefutable. A letter he wrote during the trial, to the editor of the *New York News* shows his pitifully hopeless situation. A report by his lawyer, Louis Schade, published two years after Wirz's execution, expresses Schade's belief in his innocence.

Controversy over the justice of Wirz's execution raged for many years. Jefferson Davis wrote two articles for *Belford's Magazine,* which were published in January and February 1890, exonerating Captain Wirz and proclaiming that "He died a martyr to a cause through adherence to truth." General N. P. Chipman, Judge Advocate of the military court which tried Henry Wirz, published a small volume in reply to Jefferson Davis's charges in *Belford's Magazine.* The United Daughters of the Confederacy voted to erect a monument in Wirz's memory with an inscription proclaiming him a martyr. This so aroused General Chipman that in 1911 he published a 500-page book, *The Tragedy of Andersonville,* reiterating the stand of the military commission which tried Wirz and found him guilty. And so the controversy continued into the twentieth century—Henry Wirz, Monster or Martyr?

Following is Captain Wirz's letter to the *New York News* detailing his situation and the complete text of Louis Schade's statement about his client, Henry Wirz, published April 4, 1867.

WIRZ'S LETTER TO THE NEW YORK NEWS, DETAILING HIS SITUATION.

OLD CAPITOL PRISON,
WASHINGTON CITY, D. C., *August 27th*, 1865.

To the Editor of the *New York News :*

Although a perfect stranger to you, I take, in my unfortunate and helpless condition, the liberty to address you this letter, knowing that, as a friend to the downtrodden South, you cannot but have some sympathy for a man who, as he believes, is innocently about to be sacrificed—a sympathy which I hope will prompt you to interest yourself in his behalf. I am a native of Switzerland, and, having been for years before the war a resident of Louisiana, could not do otherwise than take up arms to defend the State and country of my adoption when it was invaded. I joined the Confederate army in 1861, and served faithfully the cause I considered to be a rightful one. In 1862, the United States troops destroyed my home, and my wife and three children had to seek shelter among friends. I lost all I possessed, but a few negroes who still remained faithful. In 1864 I was ordered to report to the officer of the military prison at Andersonville, Georgia. By this officer I was put in command of the prison, and remained in that position from April 1864 until 1865. When the South ceased the struggle, I was still in Andersonville with my family, believing myself fully protected by the terms of the agreement between Generals Sherman and Johnston, and never dreaming that I, a poor captain and subaltern officer, would be made to answer with my life for what is now alleged to have been done at Andersonville. I was, in violation of a safe-conduct which was given me by a staff-officer of General Wilson, arrested in Macon, Georgia, was kept there in confinement for two weeks, and then sent on to Washington, and am now, by order of the President of the United States, brought before a court to be tried under the most atrocious charges. I have no friends here. I am helpless; and unless I can get help, will have to lose the last thing which I possess in this world—my good name and my life. My conscience is clear. I have never dealt

24

cruelly with a prisoner under my charge. If they suffered for want of shelter, food, clothing and necessaries, I could not help it, having no control over these things—things which the Confederate Government could give only in very limited quantity, even to our own men, as everybody knows who will be just and impartial. My legal advisers (Messrs. Schade and Baker) seeing my helplessness, have undertaken to conduct my defence. They are both doing it from generosity and compassion, knowing full well that I have not the means to remunerate them for their trouble. But I cannot expect them to furnish the means which it absolutely requires in the conducting of a case of such importance. Copies of depositions have to be made, messengers have to be sent here and there to get up testimony; and how can this be done without money? I have none to give; and, no doubt, my case will be lost—my life sacrificed— for want of the money to defray the expenses of such a trial. But my counsel believe, from the evidence already in their possession, that if the necessary means can be obtained, my acquittal must be the result. On this condition, I take the liberty to appeal to you to assist me, and let me not be the victim of injustice. Your influence is such that it will not require very great efforts to collect the necessary means for a vigorous carrying on of the defence. I am myself without clothes, without any means to alleviate the hardships of a close confinement. My health is bad, and the prison fare is not calculated to benefit a sick, or at least a suffering man. Still, these things I have borne without murmuring, and hope, with the help of God, to bear yet for a while longer.

Hoping that this petition will receive a favorable reception on your part, and assuring you again that nothing but the direst necessity could induce me to address you, I remain, sir, with the greatest respect, your obedient servant,

H. WIRZ,
Late Capt. and A. A. G. C. S. A.

STATEMENT PUBLISHED APRIL 4, 1867, BY LOUIS SCHADE, ATTORNEY AT LAW, WASHINGTON, D. C., WHO DEFENDED WIRZ IN HIS TRIAL.

" Intending to leave the United States for some time, I feel it my duty before I start, to fulfill in part a promise which, a few hours before his death, I gave to my unfortunate client,

25

Captain Wirz, who was executed at Washington on the 10th day of November, 1865. Protesting up to the last moment his innocence of those monstrous crimes with which he was charged, he received my word that, having failed to save him from a felon's doom, I would, as long as I lived, do everything in my power to clear his memory. I did that the more readily, as I was then already perfectly convinced that he suffered wrongfully. Since that time his unfortunate children, both here and in Europe, have constantly implored me to wipe out the terrible stains which now cover the name of their father. Though the times do not seem propitious for obtaining full justice; yet, considering that man is mortal, I will, before entering upon a perilous voyage, perform my duty to those innocent orphans, and also to myself. I will now give a brief statement of the causes which led to the arrest and execution of Captain Wirz. In April 1865, President Johnson issued a proclamation, stating that from evidence in the possession of the 'Bureau of Military Justice,' it appeared that Jefferson Davis was implicated in the assassination of Abraham Lincoln, and for that reason the President offered a reward of $100,000 on the capture of the then fugitive ex-President of the Southern Confederacy. That testimony has since been found to be entirely false and a mere fabrication, and the suborner Conover is now under sentence in the jail of this city; the two perjurers whom he suborned having turned State's evidence against him, whilst the individual by whom Conover was suborned has not yet been brought to justice.

"Certain high and influential enemies of Jefferson Davis, either then already aware of the character of the testimony of those witnesses, or not thinking their testimony quite sufficient to hang Mr. Davis, expected to find the wanting material in the terrible mortality of Union prisoners at Andersonville. Orders were issued accordingly to arrest a subaltern officer, Captain Wirz, a poor, friendless and wounded prisoner of war, (he being included in the surrender of General Johnston) and, besides, a foreigner by birth. On the 7th day of May he was placed in the Old Capitol Prison at Washington, and from that time the greater part of the Northern press was busily engaged in forming the unfortunate man, in the eyes of the Northern people, into such a monster that it became almost impossible for him to obtain counsel. Even his countryman, the Swiss Consul-general, publicly refused to accept money to defray the expenses of the trial. He was doomed before he was heard,

26

and even the permission to be heard according to law was denied him. To increase the excitement and give eclat to the proceeding, and to influence still more the public mind, the trial took place under the very dome of the Capitol of the nation. A military commission, presided over by one of the most arbitrary and despotic generals in the country, was formed; and the paroled prisoner of war, his wounds still open, and so feeble that he had to recline during the trial on a sofa. How that trial was conducted the whole world knows. The enemies of generosity and humanity believed it to be a sure thing to get at Jefferson Davis. Therefore, the first charge was that of conspiracy between Wirz, Jefferson Davis, Seddon, Howell Cobb, R. B. Winder, R. R. Stevenson, and a number of others, to kill the Union prisoners. The trial lasted for three months; but, unfortunately for the bloodthirsty instigators, not a particle of evidence was produced showing the existence of such a conspiracy, yet Captain Wirz was found guilty of that charge. Having thus failed, another effort was made. On the night before the execution of the prisoner, a telegram was sent to the Northern press from this city, stating that Wirz had made important disclosures to General L. C. Baker, the well-known detective, implicating Jefferson Davis, and that the confession would probably be given to the public. On the same evening some parties came to the confessor of Wirz, Rev. Father Boyle, and also to me, one of them informing me that a high Cabinet officer wished to assure Wirz, that if he would implicate Jefferson Davis with the atrocities committed at Andersonville, his sentence would be commuted. He, the messenger, or whoever he was, requested me to inform Wirz of this. In presence of Father Boyle I told Wirz, next morning, what had happened. The Captain simply and quietly replied: 'Mr. Schade, you know that I have always told you that I do not know anything about Jefferson Davis, he had no connection with me as to what was done at Andersonville. If I knew anything of him I would not become a traitor against him, or anybody else, even to save my life.' He likewise denied that he had ever made any statement whatever to General Baker. Thus ended the attempt to suborn Captain Wirz against Jefferson Davis. That alone shows what a man he was. How many of his defamers would have done the same? With his wounded arm in a sling, the poor paroled prisoner mounted, two hours later, the scaffold. His last words were that he died innocent; and so he did. The 10th day of November, 1865,

27

will indeed be a black stain upon the pages of American history. To weaken the effect of his declaration of innocence, and of the noble manner in which Wirz died, a telegram was manufactured here and sent North, stating that on the 27th day of October, Mrs. Wirz, (who actually was 900 miles, on that day, away from Washington) had been prevented by that Stantonian *deus ex machina*, General L. C. Baker, *from poisoning her husband*. Thus, on the same day when the unfortunate family lost their husband and father, a cowardly and atrocious attempt was made to blacken their character also. On the next day I branded the whole as an infamous lie, and since then I have never heard of it again, though it emanated from a Brigadier-general of the United States army.

"All those who were charged with having conspired with Captain Wirz have since been released, except Jefferson Davis, the prisoner of the American 'Castle Chillon.' Captain Winder was let off without trial; and if any of the others have been tried, which I do not know, certainly none of them have been hung. As Captain Wirz could not conspire alone, nobody will now, in view of that important fact, consider him guilty of that charge. So much then for charge No. I.

"As to charge No. II., to wit: Murder, in violation of the laws and customs of war,—I do not hesitate to declare what about 145 out of 160 witnesses on both sides declared during the trial, that Captain Wirz never murdered or killed any Union prisoners with his own hands or otherwise. All those witnesses (about twelve to fifteen) who testified that they saw Captain Wirz kill a prisoner, have sworn falsely; abundant proofs of that assertion being in existence. The hands of Captain Wirz are clear of the blood of prisoners of war. He would certainly have at least intimated to me a knowledge of the alleged murders with which he was charged. In almost all cases, no names of the alleged murdered men could be given; and where it was done, no such persons could be identified. The terrible scene in court when he was confronted with one of the witnesses, and the latter insisting that Wirz was the man who killed a certain Union prisoner, which irritated the prisoner so much that he almost fainted, will still be remembered. That man (Grey) swore falsely; and God alone knows what the poor, innocent prisoner must have suffered at that moment. That scene was depicted and illustrated in the Northern newspapers as if Wirz had broken down on account of his guilt. Seldom has a mortal suffered more than that friendless and forsaken man. Fearing lest this communication should be too long, I will merely speak of the principal and most intelligent of those false witnesses, who testified to individual murder on the part of Captain Wirz. Upon his testimony the Judge-advocate, in his final argument, laid particular stress, on account of his intelligence. This witness prepared also pictures of the alleged cruelties of Wirz, which were handed to the Commission, and are now on record, copies of which appeared at the time in Northern illustrated papers. He swore that his name was Felix de-la-Baume, and represented himself as a Frenchman and grand-nephew of Marquis Lafayette. After having so well testified and shown so much zeal, he received a recommendation signed by the members of the Commission. On the 11th day of October, before the taking of the testimony was concluded, he was appointed to a clerkship in the Department of the Interior. This occurred whilst one of the witnesses for the defence (Duncan) was arrested in open court and placed in prison before he had testified. After the execution of Captain Wirz, some of the Germans of Washington recognised in de-la-Baume a deserter from the Seventh New York (Steuben's) Regiment, whose name was not de-la-Baume, but Felix Oeser, a native of Saxony. They went to Secretary Harlan, and he dismissed the impostor, and the important witness in the Wirz trial, on the 21st day of November, eleven days after the execution. Nobody who is acquainted with the Conover testimony, in consequence of which the President of the United States was falsely induced to place a reward of $100,000 upon the head of an innocent man, will be astonished at the above disclosures of the character of testimony before military commissions. So much for charge II. If from twelve to fifteen witnesses could be found who were willing to testify to so many acts of murder on the part of Wirz, there must certainly have been no lack of such who were willing to swear to minor offences. Such was the unnatural state of the public mind against the prisoner at that time, that such men regarded themselves, and were regarded, as heroes, after having testified in the manner above described; whilst, on the other hand, the witnesses for the defence were intimidated, particularly after one of them had been arrested. But who is responsible for the many lives that were lost at Andersonville and in the Southern prisons? That question has not fully been settled; but history will tell on whose heads the guilt for those sacrificed hecatombs of human beings is to be placed. It was certainly not the fault of poor Captain Wirz when, in consequence of medicines having been declared contraband of war by the North, the Union prisoners died for the want of the same. How often have we read during the war that ladies going South had been arrested and placed in the Old Capitol Prison by the Union authorities, because some quinine or other medicine had been found concealed in their clothing? Our navy prevented the ingress of medical stores from the seaside, and our troops repeatedly destroyed drug-stores, and even the supplies of private physicians in the South. Thus the scarcity of medicines became general all over the South. . . .

"That provisions in the South were scarce will astonish nobody, when it is remembered how the war was carried on. General Sheridan boasted in his report that, in the Shenandoah Valley alone, he burnt over two thousand barns filled with wheat and corn, and all the mills in the whole tract of country; that he destroyed all factories of cloth, or killed and drove off every animal — even the poultry—that could contribute to human sustenance. And these desolations were repeated in different parts of the South, and so thoroughly, that last month, two years after the end of the war, Congress had to appropriate a million of dollars to save the people of those regions from actual starvation. The destruction of railroads and other means of transportation by which food could be supplied by abundant districts to those without it, increased the difficulties in giving sufficient food to our prisoners. The Confederate authorities, aware of their inability to maintain their prisoners, informed the Northern agents of the great mortality, and urgently requested that the prisoners should be exchanged, even without regard to the surplus which the Confederates had on the exchange-roll from former exchanges — that is, man for man. But our War Department did not consent to an exchange. They did not want to 'exchange skeletons for healthy men.' Finally, when all hopes of exchange were gone, Colonel Ould, the Confederate Commissioner of Exchange, offered, early in August, 1864, to deliver up all the Federal sick and wounded, without requiring an equivalent in return, and pledged that the number would amount to ten or fifteen thousand; and if it did not, he would make up that number with well men. Although this offer was made in August, the transportation was not sent for them (to Savannah) until December, although he urged and implored (to use his own words) that haste should be made. During that very

30

period the most of the deaths at Andersonville occurred. Congressman Covode, who lost two sons in Southern prisons, will do well if he inquires who those 'skeletons' were which the Hon. Secretary of War (Stanton) did not want to exchange for healthy men. If he does, he will hereafter be perhaps less bitter against the people of the South. . . .

"We used justly to proclaim in former times that ours was the 'land of the free and the home of the brave.' But when one half of the country is shrouded in a despotism which now only finds a parallel in Russian Poland; and when our generals and soldiers quietly permit that their former adversaries shall be treated worse than the Helots of old, brave soldiers though they may be, who, when the forces and resources of both sections were more equal, have not seldom seen the backs of our best generals, not to speak of such men as Butler and consorts; then we may well question whether the Star-spangled Banner still waves ' over the land of the free and the home of the brave.' A noble and brave soldier never permits his antagonist to be calumniated and trampled upon after an honorable surrender. Besides, notwithstanding the decision of the highest legal tribunal in the land that military commissions are unconstitutional, the earnest and able protestations of President Johnson, and the sad results of military commissions, yet such military commissions are again established by recent legislation of Congress all over the suffering and starving South. History is just, and, as Mr. Lincoln used to say, 'we cannot escape history.' Puritanical hypocrisy, self-adulation and self-glorification, will not save those enemies of liberty from their just punishment. Not even a Christian burial of the remains of Captain Wirz has been allowed by Secretary Stanton. They still lie side by side with those of another and acknowledged victim of military commissions, the unfortunate Mrs. Surratt, in the yard of the former jail of this city. If anybody should desire to reply to this, I politely beg that it may be done before the 1st of May next, as I shall then leave the country, to return in the fall. After that day, letters will reach me in care of the American Legation, or Mr. Benedetto Bolzani, Leipzig street No. 38, Berlin, Prussia.

"Louis Schade, *Attorney at Law.*

"Washington, D. C., *April 4th*, 1867."

Execution of Captain Henry Wirz, November 10, 1865. From Library of Congress collection.

3

The Clergy
and Andersonville Prison

L OCAL HISTORY RELATES that Robert James Hodges, master of the
Andersonville area Hodges Plantation and part-time Methodist
preacher, served as chaplain to the Confederate forces stationed at
Andersonville Prison, but there is no record whether or not he ever
tried to preach to the prisoners. History does record that the Catholic
Church sent priests to minister to the spiritual needs of Catholic
inmates.

The Reverend William John Hamilton, a Catholic priest who lived
in Macon and whose mission included all of southwestern Georgia,
visited Andersonville in May 1864. Finding a great number of Catholics
among the prisoners, he petitioned the Bishop of Savannah to send
priests to minister to them. While waiting for an answer to his request,
Father Hamilton returned to Andersonville and spent three days
giving spiritual help to Catholic inmates.

In June, Bishop Augustine Verot of Savannah sent Father Peter
Whelan to minister to Catholic prisoners of Andersonville. Finding the
needs of Catholic prisoners more than he could handle by himself,
Father Whelan wrote to Savannah for help and Father H. Claveril was
sent to assist him.

The two priests found a place to live in a shack not far from the
prison. They soon won the admiration and respect of most prisoners—
Catholics, Protestants, Jews, and atheists alike. One inmate wrote,
"They are in every day." Another wrote, "They are the only Christian
professors who visit the camp." Another inmate observed with awe that
the priests ministered to smallpox patients with the same attention
as to any other.

The priests frequently crawled on hands and knees into dugouts
to hear confessions or administer extreme unction to dying men. They
gave consolation to non-Catholics as well as Catholics and not sur-
prisingly converted many unbelievers to Catholicism. Father Claveril
soon became ill and Father John Kirby came from Augusta to replace
him, but stayed only two weeks.

Father Whelan, a man approximately 60 years of age, was upset

Execution of the Raiders, from a sketch done by James E. Taylor in 1896. Courtesy Library of Congress.

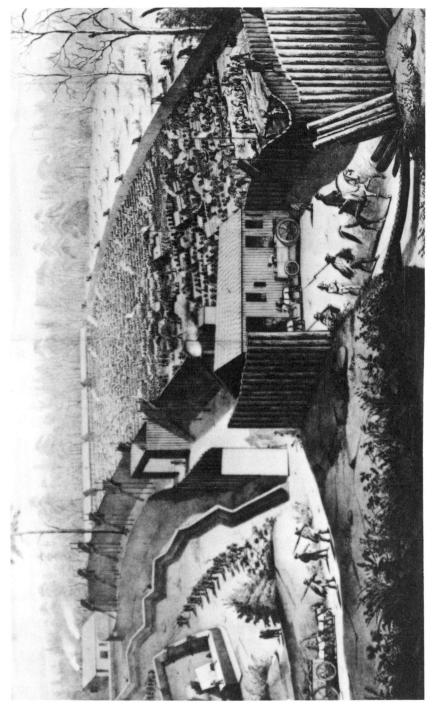

Sketch of Andersonville Prison. From collection of Library of Congress.

because there were many inmates who could not understand English. He requested that a bilingual priest be sent to assist him. A Jesuit priest from Spring Hill College near Mobile, Alabama, Father Hosannah, who could speak several languages, was sent to replace Father Kirby. He and Father Whelan remained until the end of September when most of the prisoners had been removed. Most histories of Andersonville Prison mention that Father Whelan was on hand when the infamous Raiders, a band of prisoners who attacked other prisoners, robbing the sick and dying, murdering in order to take food, clothing, and valuables from weaker men, were brought to trial at a kangaroo court inside the prison, convicted of these crimes and hanged from a gallows erected inside the stockade. Father Whelan visited these six condemned men the night before the hanging. Five of them were Catholics and received the consolation of their religion from Father Whelan. It has been recorded that during the execution the next day, Father Whelan prayed aloud.

For a period of five months from May until September 1864, Catholic prisoners at Andersonville had the support of trained spiritual guidance. Protestants did not fair so well. Although no Protestant clergy is known to have given regular service at Andersonville, a traveling Methodist missionary to Confederate troops from Florida, Reverend E. S. Duncan, stopped at Andersonville twice for the purpose of preaching the gospel to a company of Florida artillery stationed there. While there, he also preached to the prisoners. He delivered a sermon in the stockade from a box near the sutler's stand in early August 1864. Again in January 1865, when only about five thousand captives remained at Andersonville, he stopped on his way to Florida and spent three evenings conducting religious services for the Confederate troops. Before leaving, he preached to the stockade prisoners and to the patients in the prison hospital.

Rev. Duncan wrote to a fellow minister, "They listened with the most profound attention. At the close I incited them to seek religion and come to God and the ground was literally covered with them that prostrated themselves. Few in that vast assembly remained standing. They treated me with the greatest respect, thanking me kindly and begging me to return, and following me when leaving as if loath to let me go."

During the spring of 1864, perhaps getting the idea from the example of Father Whelan and his overworked assistant, Protestant prisoners who felt that their only hope was through prayer, started holding religious meetings themselves. Some of the more articulate prisoners attempted preaching. It became more or less customary to hold prayer meetings every other night. Song leaders would simply start some familiar hymn and interested prisoners would assemble. T. J. Shepherd, an Ohio prisoner who did a good deal of the preaching, later estimated that a hundred men were converted as a result of meetings with which he was connected. Also active in the services was Boston Corbett, later famous as the soldier who shot John Wilkes Booth when he was smoked out of Richard H. Garrett's barn near Fredericksburg, Virginia after his assassination of Abraham Lincoln. Out of these religious groups came an "Andersonville Sunday school" and a prisoners' organization to care for the sick and to hold funerals for those who died.

Religious Services at Andersonville

4

Andersonville Honeymoon

IT WAS RUMORED among the prisoners that a woman, masquerading as a man, was imprisoned at Andersonville and that while in the prison, she had given birth to a child. The story persisted for years after the prison was closed, but few knew whether to believe the incredible tale or not. In 1915, speculation on the subject was ended when Dr. W. J. Kerr of Corsicana, Texas, a Confederate doctor who had been stationed at Andersonville during part of the time the prison was in operation, corroborated the story in an article published in the July 1915 issue of the *Confederate Veteran.*

His story relates that in the summer of 1863, Captain Harry Hunt of Buffalo, New York, captain of a coastal vessel running out of New York City, married Miss Janie Scadden, daughter of Thomas L. Scadden of Chicago. After the wedding, Captain Hunt took his bride and a number of guests aboard his vessel for a pleasure cruise out of New York harbor. They had been out only a matter of hours when a United States revenue cutter ran across them and forced Captain Hunt to take the vessel down the coast to North Carolina for a load of corn. While loading the corn, the Confederates captured the vessel, wedding party and all. After detaining the group for several hours, all the wedding guests were turned loose, but Captain Hunt was taken into custody. His bride, thinking he'd be released in a few days, refused to leave her husband. The Confederates kept them both in confinement and later shipped both Captain Hunt and Mrs. Hunt to Andersonville Prison.

In July 1864, Dr. Kerr was ordered on duty at Andersonville to take charge of the dispensary and to superintend the building of a hospital and other government buildings connected with the prison. Dr. Kerr relates in his story: "On my arrival, I heard a very small infant crying near my office which was in the Star Fort just outside the southwest corner of the prison. On investigating, I found it was the three-day old son of Captain and Mrs. Hunt, and that the baby had been born in the prison."

Dr. Kerr visited Mrs. Hunt and found that she and Captain Hunt were living in a tent in the prison in abject poverty. Their trunk with all their clothes and five thousand dollars in greenbacks had been stolen during the thirteen months they had been imprisoned. The clothing Mrs. Hunt had left was hardly enough to keep her warm, but she had dressed the baby with some scraps she'd torn off her own clothes.

Dr. Kerr found Mrs. Hunt to be an intelligent and cultured lady in distress and he determined to help her. He persuaded all of the surgeons on the post to sign a petition to have her boarded-out at a home outside the prison. He took the petition to General Winder and after a difficult time of it, persuaded General Winder to agree to the plan. He next endeavored to find a farmhouse close by the prison where she could be boarded. This was not an easy task due to the strong feelings of people of the area, but he finally partially persuaded a farmer named Smith who agreed on the contingent that Dr. Kerr get Mrs. Smith's approval. This he managed to do. Dr. Kerr then went to Macon and persuaded a merchant friend of his to give him some remnants of calico and flannel for clothing for Mrs. Hunt and the baby. Dr. Kerr also managed to get Captain Hunt paroled and appointed a ward master in the hospital.

Dr. Kerr relates that Mrs. Hunt sent him a beautiful and touching letter of thanks and also sent him a diamond scarf pin which she had managed to keep hidden and that Captain Hunt, Mrs. Hunt, and little Harry, the baby, all survived imprisonment at Andersonville.

5

The Prison
and the Neighborhood

THE ARRIVAL OF THE first detachment of prisoners on February 15, 1864, mostly soldiers from New Hampshire, Connecticut, New Jersey, and Michigan, created unusual excitement in the region of the prison. Crowds convened at the prison daily to look through the chinks of the stockade and gaze on those within. People stood on the adjacent hills and stared, glowered, and yelled taunts to the prisoners. Old men and boys left their crops to watch the prisoners. Women left their housework. Negroes of all ages and appearance sauntered around, shouting, cheering, and wrestling with each other as on a holiday. A girls' high school, called a college in those times, one day added its whole enrollment to the crowd of spectators. The girls were taken by their teachers on an all-day excursion to Andersonville where "they chattered and stared and ate their sandwichs and took notes of what they saw as themes for their next weekly compositions," according to Ambrose Spencer in *A Narrative of Andersonville*.

Ambrose Spencer, a Yankee who lived near Americus and who in 1866 published a book dealing with his firsthand observances and his personal study of the prison and of the trial of Henry Wirz, expounds at great length on the hostile feelings of the people of the neighborhood toward the prisoners. He points out that many local preachers squelched any feelings of compassion the people might harbor toward the plight of the prisoners by preaching against pity for them and warning their congregations that rendering any sort of aid to the prisoners would be sinful.

Although Ambrose Spencer wrote at length on the hatred of the people of the community toward the prisoners, he did note some scattered instances of kindness toward prisoners by people of the community. He states that the attention of several Masonic bodies in Georgia was directed to the destitute condition of brethren of the order who were confined at Andersonville and that many Georgia Masonic Lodges took steps to relieve the wants of prisoners who were Masons. He says that the Lodges at Thomasville and Albany were conspicuous in their efforts to seek out and aid Masons in prison and hospital. Delegations from these bodies went to Andersonville and found the names of many Masons who needed their fraternal assistance. Money, clothing, and food were provided by the Albany Lodge. The Lodge at Macon contributed clothing and rendered such other services as their means permitted. Individual members of other lodges exerted themselves in the cause of humanity and did what they could to alleviate some of the suffering.

Ambrose Spencer also mentions that Dr. B. J. Head of Americus, a physician of many years' practice, who had the management of a ward in one of the hospitals at the prison, carried from his home food that his weakened patients could more easily swallow than the course prison fare—biscuits, tea, rice, vegetables, and especially tomatoes which helped his scurvy-stricken patients. Dr. Head's wife canvassed the countryside to interest the ladies of Sumter County in contributing whatever they could spare for the prisoners. Although she met with some strong opposition, she found many women willing to contribute old linen, clothes, stockings, bread, tea, coffee, and vegetables. Two lots of gifts were successfully delivered to the prison via wagons with Dr. Head, Willis Godwin, and Stephen Daniels, all of Americus, as escorts. A third shipment was stopped by the provost marshal, Lieutenant Reed, who swore he would not give a pass for "such a traitorous purpose." A group of Confederate officers not connected with the post, who were in Lieutenant Reed's office, threatened to hang Dr. Head, Daniels, and Godwin for being Yankee sympathizers. Dr. Head, who had obtained permission from General Winder for the delivery of the first two shipments, now went to General Winder's quarters to straighten things out. He found that Winder had made a complete change-about in his attitude and now declared that "not the first damned morsel shall go inside the prison!" This brought to a halt the shipments of gifts from the ladies of Sumter County, according to Ambrose Spencer.

Ambrose Spencer also tells of his own experience in aiding an escaped prisoner who was directed to Spencer's house by a friendly Negro. The escaped prisoner knocked fearfully on the Spencers' door at midnight on January 5, 1865, a bitter cold night when the mercury stood at 16 degrees. The Spencers took the Union soldier in, found he was from Lexington, Kentucky, warmed him by the fire, gave him hot coffee and a good meal, and allowed him a few hours of much needed sleep. They fitted him with warm clothing, filled his haversack with bacon, cornbread, tobacco, matches, and other provisions for a long journey, and sent him on his way with directions for getting to St. Marks, Florida where it was hoped he would find Union help.

John Lane Peek, a citizen of Andersonville at the time of the war who was born a cripple and always walked with a crutch and couldn't go into service, served as a watchman for supplies which came by train and were stockpiled out in the open not far from the depot. According to a story handed down in the Peek family and told today by Miss Nettie Mae Peek and Mrs. Clara Belle Peek Johnson, life-long residents of Andersonville, there were many packages of food and medicine addressed to prisoners and sent by the parents, wives, and relatives of prisoners, in the stockpile John Lane Peek was assigned to guard. Peek told his family that much of it didn't get any farther than this stockpile because it spoiled before Captain Wirz would allow it to be moved to the prison.

Mrs. Johnson says she remembers her father repeating what John Lane Peek had told him. of being among the crowd on the hill overlooking the stockade the day of the hanging of the six Raiders by their fellow prisoners. Five died instantly, but the rope broke before William Collins died and he fell to the ground, pleading for mercy. The rope was soon fixed and he was taken up a second time. The platform was jerked from under him and this time he died instantly of strangulation—an awful sight to see, according to Peek. John Lane Peek always thought that Collins, having been hanged by the neck once, although unsuccessfully, should not have been strung up again. This seemed to be the opinion of many who watched the hangings, including Lt. J. J. Easterlin, who was attached to the stockade command, and was a kinsman of Lewis Easterlin, present mayor of Andersonville.

During the last months of the war, after the death of General Winder, when food was so scarce that to feed the prisoners deprived the Confederates of food, and when it looked like communications between Andersonville and Richmond would soon be cut and the collapse of the Confederacy was at hand—authorities at Andersonville decided to act, without official orders, on an announcement in the newspapers of an agreement between the Confederacy and General Grant to the effect that either side might deliver to the other side on parole, but without exchange, any prisoners they chose, simply taking receipt for them. Plans were made to send 6000 prisoners to the Federals stationed at St. Augustine, Florida. An officer was sent ahead to make arrangements for the receipt of the prisoners and soon telegraphed back that he had made arrangements for the Federal commander in St. Augustine to receive them. "Send on the prisoners," he telegraphed. The prisoners were to be sent from Andersonville by rail to the Chattahoochee River and then down the river to Florida near Quincy and from Quincy by rail to Jacksonville and marched the rest of the way to St. Augustine.

A story handed down in the Easterlin family of Andersonville says that their kinsman, Lt. J. J. Easterlin, was sent along with a very few officers and guards to escort the prisoners to St. Augustine and that when this army of ragged filthy diseased prisoners arrived in St. Augustine, the Federal commander refused to receive them. The escort, on wiring this message to authorities at Andersonville, was commanded to bring the prisoners back to the prison.

Local history relates that Lt. Easterlin later told his family about the indignation of these prisoners against their own government which seemed to have abandoned them. He is reported to have said that on several occasions on the return journey, the guards closed their eyes and allowed prisoners to escape, even allowing one group to take a wagonload of corn with them—all of which seemed to make little difference in the outcome of things as the returned prisoners did not stay long at Andersonville. When news reached the prison that General Wilson with a large body of Federal cavalry was approaching Georgia from the west and that his destination was Andersonville, the authorities at the prison hastily sent the prisoners back to Jacksonville and turned them loose to make the best of their way to Federal forces at St. Augustine.

A Sumter County historian, Lloyd Caswell of Americus, tells a story passed on to him by a county resident, that Benjamin Dykes, owner of the land used for the prison site, capitalized on the fame of Providence Spring, by advertising for sale bottled Providence Spring water in Georgia and out-of-state newspapers after the war. That hermetically sealed bottles of Providence Spring water turned up in various parts of the country as late as 1896 is mentioned by John L. Maile, who as a member of Company F, Eighth Regiment, Michigan Volunteer Infantry, became a prisoner at Andersonville and survived to write a book, *Prison Life in Andersonville*. In his book, Maile tells of lecturing in Warsaw, New York in 1896 on his war and prison experiences when a local man showed him an hermetically sealed bottle of Providence Spring water obtained from a Rev. G. Stanley Lathrop of Atlanta. The water was touted as the best drinking water in all Georgia. On studying the bottle in question, Maile observed, "So pure was the content that no sediment existed."

Benjamin F. Gue, an Iowa newspaper editor who served as an Iowa state senator and as Lieutenant Governor of Iowa, claimed in a newspaper story published in the *Iowa State Register* May 30, 1884 that the state of Georgia was so ashamed of the Confederacy's treatment of prisoners at Andersonville that Andersonville disappeared from postwar maps. He wrote that while traveling through Georgia on business in 1884, he determined to visit the village of Andersonville, but when attempting to find it on a map, found that Andersonville was not to be found on any map in the South. "Southern gentlemen feign to know nothing of Andersonville. They utterly ignore its existence and assure you that its alleged horrors are Republican lies," he says. "I procured and carefully searched, not only railroad maps, but all others to be found at bookstores, and on none—not even in the railroad guides—can this place be discovered, although it is a station on the Central Railroad of Georgia. Some told me it was on the line between Georgia and South Carolina in Anderson County; others said there was no such place."

Gue found his way to Andersonville, viewed the remains of the stockade, visited the superintendent of the cemetery, and secured from him a complete roll of the Iowa soldiers who perished at Andersonville and published that roll in *The Iowa Register*. Gue returned to Andersonville in 1906 when he was principal speaker at the dedication of the Iowa Monument.

6

Clara Barton
at Andersonville

PRIVATE DORANCE ATWATER of the 2nd New York Cavalry was 18 years old when he was captured by Confederates at Hagerstown, Maryland on July 7, 1863. He was first sent to Belle Isle Prison and later transferred to Andersonville. Because of his beautiful penmanship, Atwater was put in charge of the books in which a daily record of the deaths of the prisoners was kept. Atwater soon realized that these records, which contained the name, company, regiment, and cause of death of each soldier buried there, would be invaluable to the loved ones of the deceased. In August 1864, he began to secretly copy the death list.

When he was exchanged in March 1865, Atwater hid this list, containing approximately 13,000 names, in the lining of his coat. When safely across the lines, he wrote Secretary of War Edwin Stanton, requesting a furlough of 30 days to permit him to make arrangements for the publication of his copy of the death register. Instead, he received a telegram directing him to report to the Secretary of War's office in Washington.

At the Secretary of War's office, Major Samuel Breck told Atwater, "We will give you $300 for the rolls." Atwater explained that he did not wish to sell the rolls, as he believed they should be published for the benefit of friends and relatives for whom they were copied. Breck warned that the government could confiscate the register if Atwater tried to publish the list without its sanction. He was given one day to make up his mind whether to accept Breck's offer. Atwater agreed to sell the rolls to the government for $300, a clerkship in the War Department, and the return of his register as soon as it was copied.

While waiting for the War Department to publish his rolls, Atwater read of famed Civil War nurse Clara Barton's efforts to ascertain the whereabouts of soldiers listed as missing. He wrote her, describing his rolls. Miss Barton called him to her office and said, "Tell me the whole story." She listened as Atwater described the method practiced in burial of the dead, and examined the sketch he had made of the grounds. As he talked, she became convinced of the possibility of

45

Clara Barton (Courtesy of the Library of Congress)

46

identifying the graves by comparing the numbered post marking each man's position in the burial trenches, with the corresponding number listed by the name in Atwater's register.

After talking to Atwater, Miss Barton called on Commissary-General of Prisoners Hoffman, and asked that an expedition be sent at once to Andersonville to identify, mark, and enclose the graves. This group, she said, must be accompanied by Atwater and his register. General Hoffman promised to bring the subject to Secretary of War Stanton's attention. The next day, at the Secretary's invitation, Clara Barton called at the War Department. It took Miss Barton 20 minutes to gain Stanton's approval. She was delighted when Stanton invited her to accompany the Andersonville Expedition so that she could see that her suggestions were satisfactorily carried out.

Captain James M. Moore was ordered by the Quartermaster General to proceed to Andersonville with Miss Barton, Atwater, and such other assistants as necessary. There he was "to identify, as far as possible, the graves of Union soldiers buried there, placing over them suitable memorials, and also establishing a cemetery with suitable protection to guard the graves from desecration."

To undertake the task, he was assigned 34 men (two clerks, one foreman, 12 carpenters, 12 letterers, and seven laborers) provided with materials for fencing and headboards, linseed oil, white lead, and paint brushes. By July 8, preparations had been completed, and the expedition sailed from Washington for Savannah, aboard the steamer, *Virginia.*

Clara Barton's report to the people of the United States on the subject of this Expedition to Andersonville is reproduced in its entirety here:

REPORT OF AN EXPEDITION TO ANDERSONVILLE, GEORGIA, JULY, 1865, FOR THE PURPOSE OF IDEN-TIFYING THE GRAVES AND ENCLOSING THE GROUNDS OF A CEMETERY CREATED THERE DUR-ING THE OCCUPATION OF THAT PLACE AS A PRISON FOR UNION SOLDIERS IN REBEL HANDS.

TO the People of the United States of America:

Having, by official invitation, been placed upon an expedition to Andersonville, for the purpose of identifying and marking the graves of the dead contained in those noted prison grounds, it is perhaps not improper that I make some report of the circumstances which induced the sending of such an expedition, its work, and the appearance, condition,

47

and surroundings of that interesting spot, hallowed alike by the sufferings of the martyred dead, and the tears and prayers of those who mourn them.

During a search for the missing men of the United States Army, commenced in March, 1865, under the sanction of our late lamented President Lincoln, I formed the acquaintance of Dorence Atwater, of Connecticut, a member of the 2nd New York Cavalry, who had been a prisoner at Belle Isle and Andersonville twenty-two months, and charged by the Rebel authorities with the duty of keeping the Death Register of the Union prisoners who died amid the nameless cruelties of the last-named prison.

By minute inquiry, I learned from Mr. Atwater the method adopted in the burial of the dead; and by carefully comparing his account with a draft which he had made of the grounds appropriated for this purpose by the Prison authorities, I became convinced of the possibilities of identifying the graves, simply by comparing the numbered post or board marking each man's position in the trench in which he was buried, with the corresponding number standing against his name upon the register kept by Mr. Atwater, which he informed me was then in the possession of the War Department.

Assured by the intelligence and frankness of my informant of the entire truthfulness of his statements, I decided to impart to the officers of the Government the information I had gained, and accordingly brought the subject to the attention of General Hoffman, Commissary-General of prisoners, asking that a party or expedition be at once sent to Andersonville, for the purpose of identifying and marking the graves and enclosing the grounds; and that Dorence Atwater, with his register, accompany the same, as the proper person to designate and identify. The subject appeared to have been not only unheard, but unthought of; and from the generally prevailing impression that no care had been taken in the burial of our prisoners, the idea seemed at first difficult to be entertained. But the same facts which had served to convince me presented themselves favorably to the good understanding and kind heart of General Hoffman, who took immediate steps to lay the matter before the Hon. Secretary of War, upon whom, at his request, I called the following day, and learned from him that he heard and approved my proposition, and decided to order an expedition consisting of materials and men, under charge of some Government officer, for the accomplishment of the objects set forth in my request, and invited me to accompany the expedition in person, which invitation I accepted.

Accordingly, on the 8th of July, the propeller Virginia, having on board fencing material, head boards, the prison records, forty workmen, clerks and letterers, under command of Captain James M. Moore, A. Q. M., Dorance Atwater and myself, left Washington for Andersonville, via Savannah, Georgia, arriving at the latter place July 12th. Having waited at Savannah seven days, and then resumed the journey by way of Augusta, Atlanta, and Macon, the entire party reached its destination in safety about noon on the 25th of July.

We found the prison grounds, stockade, hospital sheds, and the various minor structures, almost in the same condition in which they had been evacuated; and care is taken to leave these historic monuments undisturbed, so long as the elements will spare them.

There is not, and never was, any town or village at this place except what grew out of its military occupation. Anderson Station, on the railroad from Macon to Eufala, was selected as a depot for prisoners, probably on account of its remoteness and possible security, and the prison itself, with the buildings which sprang up around it, constituted all there was of Andersonville.

The land around it is broken and undulating, and at the time of the occupation was covered with forests, mostly of the long-leafed pine, common to the uplands of the South. The bases of the hills are lined with cozy springs, which unite to form little rivulets, one of which winds sluggishly through each of the intervening marshy alleys.

The original enclosure of 19 acres was made in the unbroken woods; and the timber was only removed as it was wanted for the necessities of the prison. The enclosure was made in January, 1864, and enlarged during the summer to 25¾ acres, being a quadrangle of 1,295 by 865 feet. The greatest length is from north to south, the ground rising from the middle toward each end in rather a step, rounded hill, the northern one being at once the highest and of the greatest extent. A small stream, rising from springs a little to the eastward, flows across it through a narrow valley filled with a compost washed down by the rains. The enclosing stockades is formed of pine logs, 20 feet in length and about eight inches in diameter, sunk five feet in the ground, and placed close together. This is again surrounded by two successive and precisely similar palisades—a portion of the last of which is gone. It seems never to have been completed. The two inner walls remain entire. With the interior space, at the distance of about 17 feet from the stockade, runs the famous dead line, marked by small posts set in the ground, and a slight of pine boards nailed on the top of them. The gates, of which there are two, situated on the west side, were continuations of the stockade, enclosing spaces of 30 feet square, more or less, with massive doors at either end. They were arranged and worked on the principle of canal locks. Upon the inner stockade were 52 sentry boxes, raised above the top of the palisades, and accessible to the guard by ladders. In these stood 52 guards, with loaded arms, so near that they could converse with each other. In addition to these, seven forts mounted with field artillery, commanded the fatal space and its masses of perishing men.

Under the most favorable circumstances, and best possible management, the supply of water would have been insufficient for half the number of persons who had to use it. The existing arrangements must have aggravated the evil to the utmost extent. The sole establishment for cooking and baking were placed on the bank of the stream immediately above and between the two inner lines of palisades. The grease and refuse from them were found adhering to the banks at the time of our visit. The guards, to the number of about 3,000, were principally encamped on the upper part of the stream, and when the heavy rains washed down the hill-sides, covered with 30,000 human beings, and the outlet below failed to discharge the flood which backed up and filled the valley, the water must have become so foul and loathsome that every statement I have seen of its offensiveness must be considered as falling short of the realty. And yet within rifle shot of the prison there flowed a stream 15 feet wide and three feet deep of pure, delicious water. Had the prison been placed so as to include a section of the "Sweet Water Creek," the inmates might have drank and bathed to their hearts' content.

During the occupation, a beautiful spring broke out like the waters of Meribah from the solid ground, near the foot of the northern slope, just under the western dead-line. It is still there—cool and clear—the only pleasing object in this horrid place.

The scarcity of water, the want of occupation, and perhaps the desire to escape by tunneling, impelled the prisoners to dig wells. Forty of these, finished and unfinished, remain. Those on the highest ground being sunk in the hard soil to the depth of eighty feet. The work was done with knives, spoons, sticks, and other tools but little better. The diggers brought up the earth in their pockets and blouses, and sprinkled it around the ground to conceal the quantity. In some wells excellent water was reached, and in others, horizontal galleries were attempted, for escape. In at least one instance, a tunnel was carried entirely through the hill, and a few prisoners are said to have got through.

The steep face of the northern hill is burrowed throughout its whole extent. The little caves are scooped out and arched in the form of ovens, floored, ceiled and strengthened so far as the owners had means, with sticks and pieces of boards, and some of them are provided with fire-places and chimneys. It would seem that there were cases, during long rains, where the house would become the grave of its owner, by falling in upon him in the night. In these burrows are still found remnants of the wretched food and rude utensils of the occupants—drinking cups made of sections of horns, platters and spoons wrought from parts of old canteens, kettles and pans made, without solder, from stray pieces of tin or sheet iron. I brought away a considerable number of these articles, which may one day be of interest to the curious.

Five sheds stand on the top of the northern hill, erected in the early part of the occupation, and five more on the opposite height, built a short time before the evacuation.

Like nearly all southern land, the soil is liable to be washed away by the rains, and on the slopes of the hills, ravines are now formed, gullied to the depth of 12 feet. It seems impossible that men could have kept their footing on these hillsides when slippery with rain.

Outside the enclosure and nearly parallel with its south end, is the hospital stockade—600 feet by 350 feet. It contains 22 sheds, for the most part without sides, erected about three months before the place was abandoned. The old hospital, occupied up to that time, in which so many brave men died, consisted only of tents enclosed by a board fence, and surrounded by a guard. Confused heaps of rubbish alone mark the place it occupied.

About half a mile from the main prison, and near Anderson Station, is the officers' stockade,—a small enclosure, in which were never imprisoned more than 250 officers—and it was chiefly used for the confinement of rebel offenders.

The Cemetery, around which the chief interest must gather, is distant about 300 yards from the stockade in a north-westerly direction. The graves, placed side by side in close continuous rows, cover nine acres, divided into three unequal lots by two roads which intersect each other

50

nearly at right angles. The fourth space is still unoccupied, except by a few graves of "Confederate" soldiers.

No human bodies were found exposed, and none were removed. The place was found in much better condition than had been anticipated, owing to the excellent measures taken by Major-General Wilson, commanding at Macon, and a humane, public-spirited citizen of Fort Valley, Georgia, a Mr. Griffin, who in passing on the railroad, was informed by one of the ever-faithful negroes that the bodies were becoming exposed, and were rooted up by animals. Having verified this statement, he collected a few negroes, sank the exposed bodies, and covered them to a proper depth. He then reported the facts to General Wilson, and requested authority to take steps for protecting the grounds. That patriotic officer visited Andersonville in person, appointed Mr. Griffin temporary Superintendent, and gave him such limited facilities as could be furnished in that destitute country. It was determined to enclose a square of fifty acres; and at the time of our arrival, the fence was nearly one-third built,—from old lumber found about the place. He had also erected a brick-kiln, and was manufacturing brick for drains to conduct the water away from the graves, and protect and strengthen the soil against the action of heavy rains. We found Mr. Griffin, with a force of about 20 negroes and a few mules, at work on the grounds. I have understood that that gentleman furnished the labor at his own cost, while General Wilson issued the necessary rations.

The part performed by our party was to take up and carry forward the work so well commenced. Additional force was obtained from the military commandant at Macon for completing the enclosure and erecting the head-boards. It seems that the dead had been buried by Union prisoners, paroled from the stockade and hospital for that purpose. Successive trenches, capable of containing from 100 to 150 bodies each, and thickly set with little posts or boards, with numbers in regular order carved upon them, told to the astonished and tear-dimmed eye the sad story of buried treasures. It was only necessary to compare the number upon each post with that which stands opposite the name on the register, and replace the whole with a more substantial, uniform and comely tablet, bearing not only the original number, but the name, company and regiment, and date of death of the soldier who slept beneath.

I have been repeatedly assured by prisoners that great care was taken at the time by the men to whom fell the sad task of originally marking this astonishing number of graves, to perform the work with faithfulness and accuracy. If it shall prove that the work performed by those who followed, under circumstances so much more favorable, was executed with less faithfulness and accuracy than the former, it will be a subject of much regret—but unfortunately not yet beyond the possibility of correction. The number of graves marked is 12,920. The original records, captured by General Wilson, furnished about 10,500, but as one book of the record had not been secured, over 2,000 names were supplied from a copy (of his own record) made by Mr. Atwater in the Andersonville Prison, and brought by him to Annapolis, on his return with the paroled prisoners.

Interspersed throughout this death register were 400 numbers against which stood only the dark word "unknown." So scattered among the thickly designated graves, stand 460 tablets, bearing only the number and the touching inscription "Unknown Union Soldier."

Substantially, nothing was attempted beyond enclosing the grounds, identifying and marking the graves, placing some appropriate mottoes at the gates and along the spaces designed for walks, and erecting a flagstaff in the center of the cemetery. The work was completed on the 17th of August, and the party took the route homeward by way of Chattanooga, Nashville, and Cincinnati, arriving at Washington on the morning of August 24th.

The health of the party during the expedition was remarkably good, when the season of the year, the fatigue, and the want of customary accommodations are taken into consideration. Cases of slight chills and fevers were not infrequent; but during the entire time, we had only one case of severe illness, and that, to our grief, terminated fatally. Edward Watts, of Georgetown, S. C., a clerk in the Q. M. Department in this city, sickened of typhoid fever during the passage up the Savannah River, and died on the 16th day of August. His remains were taken home to his friends.

Mr. Watts was a young man of education and refinement, and of the highest type of moral and religious character; he suffered patiently and died nobly and well. I have thought that he might be regarded as the last martyr of Andersonville.

The future of this historic spot cannot fail to constitute a subject of deep and abiding interest to the people of this entire country, and it would seem fitting that it should be preserved as one of the sanctuaries of the nation, and be in due time decorated with appropriate honors. The susceptibility of internal improvement is very great. Water can be had for irrigation, and the climate will produce nearly all the flora of the temperate zones. Both national gratitude and personal affection will suggest the erection of a suitable monument within the cemetery, where, if desirable, may be preserved in durable form the names of the martyrs who sleep around. And as the land on which all these interesting associations are clustered is still the property of private individuals, never having passed from the hands of the original owners, it would seem desirable that the cemetery, at least, and its immediate surroundings, become the property of the nation. A mile square will embrace all points of general and historic interest.

There are numerous smaller burial places in the State of Georgia, which from their seeming lesser importance, will scarcely be kept up as national cemeteries, and in reference to which, without venturing to suggest, I would merely remark that the 50 acres enclosed at Andersonville would afford ample space for all whom it might ever be deemed advisable to remove to that point.

During the occupation of Andersonville as a prison, it was a punishable offense for a colored man or woman to feed, shelter, aid, or even converse with a prisoner on parole. To others they had no access. I have been informed that they were not allowed about the prison grounds; and so great was their superstititous horror of the cruelties perpetrated upon the prisoners that only a comparatively small number had ever found the courage to visit the cemetery up to the time of our arrival. But the presence of so many northern people on such an errand, and especially a lady, entirely overcame their fears, and they visited the cemetery and myself by scores, men, women and children, sometimes 100 in a day. It was no uncommon occurrence, upon opening my tent in the morning to find a group standing in front of it, who had walked 15 or 20 miles to see the "Yankee lady" and ask her "if it were true that Abraham Lincoln was dead, and they were free," and "how Massa Lincoln's great paper read," and "what they ought to do," and tell her how the "poor Yankee prisoners" ran before the dogs, "like us" and they could not save them—starved, and they could not feed them—died, and they could not see them.

Remember, mothers, that the pitying tear of the old-time slave, whom your son helped to freedom, is the only tear that falls upon his distant grave today.

I have endeavored to point out to you, as faithfully as I am able, the various objects of interest, painful or otherwise, which presented themselves to my observation during the time occupied in the work of the expedition; and while I would not dwell upon the terribleness of the sufferings imposed upon our prisoners, nor stir the hearts already sunk in grief to deeper woe, still we owe it alike to the living and the dead, that a proper knowledge and a realization of the miseries which they endured be entertained by all. We are wont to attribute their chief suffering to insufficiency of food, and while this is probably just, still, to the mind of one who has looked over the scanty, shelterless, pitiful spot of earth to which they were confined, and taken into consideration the numberless trials which must have grown out of the privation of space and the necessary conveniences of life, the conviction will force itself that these latter woes fell but little short of the former. It is to be remembered that during 13 long months, they knew neither shelter nor protection from the changeable skies above, nor the pitiless unfeeling earth beneath.

The treacherous nature of the soil, parching to seams in the sun, and the gullying and sliding under their feet with every shower, must have augmented their ills almost beyond conception. I watched the effect of a heavy fall of rain upon the enclosed grounds, and in 30 minutes the entire hill sides, which had constituted their sole abiding place, were one rolling mass of slippery mud, and this the effect of a mere summer shower. What of the continuous rains of Autumn? Think of 30,000 men penned by close stockade upon 26 acres of ground, from which every tree and shrub had been uprooted for fuel to cook their scanty food, huddled like cattle, without shelter or blanket, half-clad and hungry, with the dreary night setting in, after a day of Autumn rain. The hill tops would not hold them all, the valley was filled with the swollen brook; 17 feet from the stockade ran the fatal dead line, beyond which no man might step and live. What did they do? I need not ask where did they go, for on the face of the whole earth, green as it was, there was no place but this for them; but where did they place themselves? How did they live? Ay, how did they die? But this is only one feature of their suffering, and perhaps the lightest. Of the long dazzling months when gaunt famine stalked at noonday, and pestilence walked by night, and upon the seamed and parching earth the cooling rains fell not, I will not trust me to speak. I scarce dare think. If my heart were strong enough to draw the picture, there are thousands upon thousands all through our land too crushed and sore to look upon it. But after this, whenever any man who has lain a prisoner within the stockade at Andersonville, would tell you of his sufferings, how he fainted, scorched, drenched, hungered, sickened, was scoffed, scourged, hunted and persecuted, though the tale be long and twice told, as you would have your own wrongs appreciated, your own woes pitied, your own cries for mercy heard, I charge

53

Entrance to Andersonville Prison Park.

A portion of the almost 13,000 graves of Union soldiers who perished at Andersonville.

Burying the dead at Andersonville. From National Archives Collection.

you listen and believe him. However definitely he may have spoken, or deeply he may have colored his picture, know that the realty calls for a better light, and a nearer view than your clouded, distant gaze will ever get. And your sympathies need not be confined to Andersonville, while similar horrors glared in the sunny light, and spotted the flower-girt garden fields of that whole, desperate, misguided and bewildered people. Wherever stretched the form of a Union prisoner, there rose the signal for cruelty and the cry of agony, and there, day by day, grew the skeleton graves of the nameless dead.

But braving and enduring all this, some thousands have returned to you. And you will bear with me and with these noble men will pardon me, while in conclusion, I speak one word of them.

The unparalleled severities of our four years' campaigns have told upon the constitutional strength even of the fortunate soldier, who marched to the music of the Union, and slept only beneath the folds of the flag for which he fought. But they whom fickle fortune left to crouch at the foot of the shadowless palmetto and listen to the hissing of the serpent, drank still deeper of the unhealthful draught. These men bear with them the seeds of disease and death, sown in that fatal clime, and ripening for an early harvest. With occasional exceptions, they will prove to be short-lived and enfeebled men, and whether they ask it or not, will deserve at your hands no ordinary share of kindly consideration. The survivor of a rebel prison has endured and suffered what you never can, and what, I pray God, your children never may. With less of strength, and more of sad and bitter memories, he is with you now, to earn the food so long denied him. If he ask "leave to toil," give it to him before it is too late; if he need kindness and encouragement, bestow them freely, while you may; if he seek charity at your hands, remember that "the poor you have always with you," but him you have not always, and withhold it not. If hereafter you find them making organized effort to provide for the widow and orphan of the Union prisoner, remember that it grows out of the heart sympathy which clusters around the memories of the comrades who perished at their side, and a well-grounded apprehension for the future of their own, and aid them.

In conclusion, tremulously, lest I assume too much, let me hasten to recommend to the grateful consideration of this noble, generous people, alike the soldier who has given his strength, the prisoner who has sacrificed his health, the widow who has offered up her husband, the orphan that knows only that its father went out to battle and comes no more forever, and the lonely distant grave of the martyr, who sleeps alone in a stranger soil, that freedom and peace might come to ours.

One word of explanation, in conclusion, and I have done. You have longed and justly felt that some report of this expedition, embracing a record of the graves identified and reclaimed, was due you. And 3,000 letters addressed to me upon the subject have revealed only too plainly and painfully the bitter anxiety with which you have watched and waited.

A mere report, accompanied by the "record" seemed a hollow mockery, which I would not impose upon you, and this is my first opportunity for such accompaniment. For the record of your dead you are indebted to the forethought, courage and perseverance of Dorance Atwater, a young man not yet 21 years of age; an orphan, four years a soldier; one-tenth part of his whole life a prisoner, with broken health and ruined hopes, he seeks to present to your acceptance the sad gift he has in store for you; and grateful for the opportunity, I hasten to place beside it this humble report whose only merit is its truthfulness, and beg you to accept it in the spirit of kindness in which it is offered.

CLARA BARTON.

New Jersey erected the first of 15 state monuments in 1899.

7

The Trials
of the Wirz Monument

In 1905, the Georgia Division of the United Daughters of the Confederacy voted to erect a monument to the memory of Captain Henry Wirz, executed keeper of the Andersonville prison. This action brought forth a tumult of passionate controversy which reached across the nation and blocked for four years the placing of such a monument at Andersonville.

At the 14th annual convention of the Georgia Division of the UDC held in Savannah in 1908, the Daughters had still not decided what to do with their $2000 granite monument which was completed, ready for erection, and languishing in Harrold Brothers Warehouse in Americus, Georgia. Miss Alice Baxter of Atlanta, president, addressed the convention on the subject. "We Georgia Daughters of the Confederacy have determined upon a monument in memory of Captain Henry Wirz, both as a vindication of the Confederacy's treatment of her prisoners of war, and as a protest against the unfair trial and unjust execution by the United States Government, of this unfortunate man. The movement was undertaken during the administration of Mrs. A. B. Hall through resolutions introduced by Mrs. Mary L. Young, Miss Anna C. Benning and Mrs. C. C. Sanders. From the time our purpose became known we have met with vehement protest on the part of the North, usually taking the form of bitter invective—sometimes, that of earnest pleading—from such Northerners as can agree to disagree.

"We counted this Wirz monument as belonging to Georgia, but since its building has become a matter of almost national interest, we take broader grounds. As Americans, as well as Georgians, we deplore that dark page in American history on which is recorded the execution of Captain Wirz. This Government is our Government. Our Georgia boys are following the American flag. We sent more men to the Spanish American War, in proportion to our population, than any other state in the Union. We were under the American flag on November 10th, 1865, the date of the Captain Wirz execution. We have a right to lament the action of our Government in a matter wherein we believe wrong was done, however long ago.

"We, the peaceful women of a peaceful time, are so convinced of our right understanding of the facts concerning Andersonville prison that we hope for dispassionate historians of the future to come to Georgia's understanding of the facts and to realize how the policy of the United States Government crowded that prison at a time when the Confederate Government confessed inability to care for the prisoners, and to further realize the terrible injustice of having held one man, and he a subordinate officer, responsible for the awful conditions existing there.

"The resolutions for building the Wirz Monument called for its erection at Andersonville. Since the acceptance of these resolutions, many of you have come seriously to question the wisdom of this location. A majority of our chapters have asked for a postponement of the unveiling to allow opportunity at this Convention for reconsidering the placing of the monument at Andersonville. I trust you may be guided to a right decision."

The proposal for placing a monument in Andersonville to the memory of Henry Wirz was attacked by newspapers in both the North and the South. Hundreds of letters were received by Georgia Division UDC leaders, protesting the erection of the monument at Andersonville. Many letters pointed out that thousands of Northerners and Southern Negroes assembled in Andersonville every May on the last weekend of that month for Memorial Day exercises and that the order of these assemblages was bad, that drunkenness was usually rampant and that in the past killings had taken place. The Georgia Division of the UDC was warned that the Wirz monument would undoubtedly incite anger among these people and that they might take out their anger by desecrating the monument. Federal authorities at the Andersonville National Cemetery would not agree to the placing of the monument inside the cemetery or Prison Park and they deplored the idea that the monument might be placed anywhere in or near Andersonville. Wishing to deter the Daughters from placing the monument in the Andersonville area, they offered to take down signs and placards derogatory to the Confederacy and the South which had been posted in the cemetery and which had aroused the ire of the Georgia Division of the UDC.

And so the movement to erect a monument to Henry Wirz at Andersonville came up for reconsideration by the 1908 Georgia Division's annual convention. Andersonville as a site for the monument was withdrawn, the unveiling ceremonies were postponed, and the floor was thrown open for consideration of other sites, Americus, county seat of Sumter County in which Andersonville is located, offered a si`e gratis. Macon delegates pled that the monument be placed on the Wesleyan College campus. Savannah wanted the monument, and Richmond delegates argued that as the former capital of the Confederacy, the Wirz Monument should be located there. After hot debate, Richmond was selected by a majority vote. A committee was appointed to secure a site in Richmond and to arrange for transportation of the monument from Americus to Richmond. This is how matters stood at the close of the 1908 Georgia Division UDC Convention.

At the 1909 convention, the Richmond committee reported it had secured a site in the Hollywood Cemetery in Richmond and was in the process of arranging for transportation—but the Georgia Division had second thoughts about sending their Wirz monument out of the state.

At the request of 66 Georgia chapters, an extra session of the 1909 convention was called for March 11 for the purpose of considering more fully the location of the Wirz monument. The action of the 1908 convention which tendered the Wirz monument to Richmond, was rescinded by a majority vote and the hotly debated question of where the monument would finally be erected narrowed down to Andersonville, Americus, or Macon. Mrs. Algernon F. Hodges of the Hodges Plantation near Andersonville, was one of the speakers at this session,

United Daughters of the Confederacy Georgia Division leaders pose for photograph at May 12, 1909 dedication of Wirz Monument.

speaking in favor of Andersonville as the proper location for the monument. The question was finally decided in favor of Andersonville.

The inscription committee which had kept its deliberations secret through many months of consultations, read to the 1909 convention the inscriptions which would be on four sides of the 45-foot high obelisk shaft.

ON FRONT

In memory of Captain Henry Wirz, C.S.A. Born Zurich, Switzerland, 1822. Sentenced to death and executed at Washington, D. C., Nov. 10, 1865.

"To rescue his name from the stigma attached to it by embittered prejudice, this shaft is erected by the Georgia Division, United Daughters of the Confederacy."

ON SECOND SIDE

Discharging his duty with such humanity as the harsh circumstances of the times, and the policy of the foe permitted, Captain Wirz became at last the victim of a misdirected popular clamor.

He was arrested in time of peace, while under the protection of a parole, tried by a military commission of a service to which he did not belong and condemned to ignominious death on charges of excessive cruelty to Federal prisoners. He indignantly spurned a pardon, proffered on condition that he would incriminate President Davis and thus exonerate himself from charges of which both were innocent.

THIRD SIDE

"It is hard on our men held in Southern prisons not to exchange them, but it is humanity to those left in the ranks to fight our battles. At this particular time to release all rebel prisoners North, would insure Sherman's defeat and would compromise our safety here."

August 18, 1864.

ULYSSES S. GRANT

FOURTH SIDE

"When time shall have softened passion and prejudice, when reason shall have stripped the mask of misrepresentation, then justice, holding even her scales, will require much of past censure and praise to change places."

December, 1888.

JEFFERSON DAVIS

When the special session decided upon the center of the tiny town of Andersonville as the site, the Daughters moved swiftly toward the erection of the monument. Wednesday, May 12, 1909 at 10 a.m. was set for the unveiling ceremonies.

UDC monument to Capt. Henry Wirz which stands in center of town of Andersonville.

Two special trains were reserved to take UDC delegates, Confederate veterans, and Southern dignitaries from Americus to Andersonville. A crowd of approximately 4000 assembled for the proceedings at which Pleasant A. Stovall, editor of the *Savannah News* and Dr. J. C. Olmstead of Atlanta were principal speakers. Henry Wirz's daughter, Mrs. J. S. Perrin of Mississippi and her small daughter, Gladys, had the honor of doing the unveiling. The Perrins had been brought to Georgia at the expense of the UDC Georgia Division and while in Andersonville were guests at the nearby Hodges Plantation.

The day of the dedication was unusually cold for May, but a good portion of the crowd stayed for the outdoor pork barbecue dinner served in the pecan orchard next to the Joel English home. (This was a log house, located adjacent to the Andersonville Methodist Church, where the Leon Holloways reside today.)

Mrs. Clara Belle Peek Johnson, 77-year-old life-long resident of Andersonville, remembers that the men of the town stayed up most of the previous night barbecuing the hogs and the ladies made salads, cakes and pies for the dinner. Long wooden tables were set up next to Joel English's house and she remembers that a detachment of Federal soldiers was present. She also remembers the soldiers stacking their rifles before sitting down to eat.

The controversial monument stands in the center of the town of Andersonville to this day. In 1919, the monument was defaced with yellow and black paint. The deed was attributed to United States airmen stationed at Souther Field near Americus. There is a favorite story told by UDC ladies of Americus about how their Wirz Monument was cleaned of the defacing paint. It seems that many people of Americus extended courtesies to the personnel of Souther Field, that Americus belles, chaperoned by Americus matrons, had attended dances at the Field, and that in return Americus society had entertained Souther Field military men at dances and parties. Mrs. Frank Harrold, an Americus matron and state officer of UDC, on hearing of the desecration of the Wirz Mounment, asked the commanding officer of Souther Field if she might address an assemblage of the entire personnel of the Field. The men were assembled, and Mrs. Harrold politely but firmly announced that Americus homes and Americus civic parties would be closed to Souther Field personnel and that no Americus belles would attend Souther Field dances until the defacing paint was removed from the Wirz Monument. By the close of the following day, every trace of paint had been scrubbed off and the monument was restored to its former condition. Military authorities at Souther Field immediately investigated the matter of the desecration of the

Andersonville Depot, early twentieth century.

Andersonville residents still vote in this century-old building.

monument and three soldiers were charged with the deed. Unfortunately two of the men had since been discharged and had returned to their homes in California, but punishment was meted out by the military to the unfortunate offender still in the service.

At the time of the dedication of the monument, the highway between Americus and Oglethorpe swung through the center of Andersonville and all through-traffic had to go around the Wirz Mounment. Large trucks swinging around the town square, sometimes grazed the base of the monument, chipping and cracking the granite. Naturally, as the years went by, dirt and stains accumulated, threatening to obilterate the inscriptions. In 1958, the Georgia Division of the Daughters of the Confederacy sponsored a bill in the Georgia Legislature to have the Georgia Historical Commission finance the repairing and cleaning of the Wirz Monument. This brought forth some heated debate in the Georgia House of Representatives. Seventy-year-old Representative U. S. Lancaster of Jones County, whose uncle had been a Confederate guard at Andersonville Prison, spoke out vehemently against the proposal. He declared, "Wirz was abhorred by the Confederate veterans themselves and was as cruel as any man that ever lived." Largely becausee of Representative Lancaster's indignation, the bill was defeated.

8

The Freedman's School

O N OCTOBER 29, 1866, about a year and a half after the cessation of the Civil War, a school for the children and the grandchildren of freed slaves was established near Andersonville under the auspices of the Congregational Society of Barrington, Rhode Island.

The school originally consisted of two large wooden buildings— the abandoned buildings of the old Confederate Hospital, southwest of the prison. One building was used as the teacherage and the other as the schoolhouse.

The school was started with two white teachers and about 63 black boys and girls. The teachers were generally shunned by the white population of Andersonville. By 1867, there was a night school as well as a day school. Miss Mary L. Battey was the day school teacher. Her report for April 1867 lists 23 male and 43 female pupils. Miss Maria L. Root, the night school teacher, listed 28 male and 8 female students—the majority over 16 years of age. The school was in part supported with financial donations by the pupils. In Miss Battey's and Miss Root's report to the District Superintendent of Freedman's Schools, $27.75 was the total amount paid by the pupils for the month of April 1867.

The American Missionary Normal School, as the Freedman's School was called, was in operation until about 1920. Some years after its beginning in the abandoned Confederate Hospital, it must have been moved a few miles west to Freedman's Hill as older citizens of Andersonville remember that the school was located on the hill around the turn of the century. A Congregational Mission Church was also built on Freedman's Hill. Area citizens say that Freedman's Hill got its name because after the War, the Federal government acquired a tract of land there and divided it into 40-acre farms and offered them as homesteads to freed slaves.

One of the school's graduates was "Miss Janie" Tondee Cotton who became a teacher in the Sumter County School System where she served for 40 years. Janie Tondee was born on the Robert Hodges Plantation where her mother, Lizzy Tondee, was a fieldhand. Her grandfather, Eliza Tondee, had been a slave and had acquired a 40-acre homestead on Freedman's Hill after the War.

Janie entered the mission school in 1904. When she attended the school, there were about 250 pupils and three teachers. "The faculty was integrated," she said in an interview with this writer in 1971, about a year before her death at the age of 74. "I remember a white teacher from the North, Miss Wilcox, and a black teacher whose name was Miss Buford. Reverend Ralph Johnson, Negro, became principal while I was there. He was also the preacher of the mission Congregational Church on Freedman's Hill. His wife became one of the teachers at the school."

"Reverend Johnson taught us Bible and arithmetic," recalled Miss Janie. "His wife tried to explain the War Between the States. We also had reading, spelling, writing, and health lessons. The girls were given quilting material each morning to work on any time during the day when their group was not having a lesson. Each girl eventually had a quilt to take home. The boys made washboards and cornshuck mops when not engaged in lessons. Each pupil paid 50¢ a month tuition."

Janie Tondee graduated from the Andersonville Freedman's School when she had completed the tenth grade. (In those days, Georgia high schools seldom boasted eleventh or twelfth grades.) At the age of fifteen, she secured a job as a teacher by going a few miles over the county line to the Macon County Superintendent of School's office in the town of Oglethorpe and taking an exam. Her first assignment was in a rural Macon County school six miles from Andersonville where she was the entire faculty teaching all grades, one through seven. After four years in Macon County, she spent forty-one years as a Sumter County teacher, the last twenty-seven years at Union Oak Grove School on the edge of the Hodges Plantation where she was born. She spent most of her summers at either Fort Valley State College or State Teachers and Agricultural College at Forsyth working to improve her teaching skills.

Mrs. Robert Hodges, who was always very much interested in Miss Janie's career and who encouraged her through the years, says, "She was liked and respected by all the townspeople, black and white alike, all of whom addressed her as 'Miss Janie.' She went beyond the teaching of the required reading, writing, and arithmetic and stressed good citizenship. She taught all the girls Home-Demonstration-Agent-approved cooking methods and sewing. She taught the boys the rudiments of cooking and also carpentry and woodworking. Right up until her death at the age of 74, she preached the value of an education to all the young people of her community. She helped many young blacks receive financial aid for a college education through a college fund she established in Negro churches of the area."

Miss Janie always said that as a child she was awe-struck by the teachers at the Freedman's School. She modeled her life after those teachers, trying to continue with the work they had started at the mission school.

9

Hodges Plantation

T WO MILES SOUTH of the Andersonville Prison grounds is the 131-year-old two-story plantation home of Mrs. R. J. Hodges. The imposing old frame home, built with slave labor in 1842, has stood silent witness to the history of Andersonville Prison and the events which followed.

Being the largest plantation in the area and the one nearest to the prison, the Hodges Plantation and the people who lived there at the time were bound to have had a part in the chaotic history of the prison. Robert James Hodges, first master of the plantation, set aside 60 acres of vegetables, mostly sweet potatoes and corn, for the use of the prisoners. Anna Hodges, grown daughter of the household, told of paroled prisoners coming to the plantation for wagonloads of fresh produce. She and the other women of the household often gave these prisoners cloth to be used to patch their tattered uniforms. General John H. Winder, Captain Henry Wirz, and Confederate officers on the stockade commander's staff were sometimes dinner guests in the home. During the trial of Henry Wirz, when it was first intimated that someone from Andersonville would be ordered to Washington as a witness in the case, one of the citizens of the neighborhood said, "Judge Hodges, you will be summoned." Judge Hodges replied, "Never! For I would give too plain and fair a statement to please his accusers."

A generation later, Mrs. Algernon F. Hodges, daughter-in-law of Judge Robert James Hodges, was instrumental in the efforts of the United Daughters of the Confederacy to locate the Wirz monument in Andersonville and Henry Wirz's daughter, Mrs. J. S. Perrin, was the Hodges' house guest while in Andersonville for the dedication of that monument. Today, Mrs. R. J. Hodges, whose husband ran the plantation for 50 years until his death in 1971, is active in the Sumter Historic Preservation Society's efforts to develop Andersonville historic sites.

Robert James Hodges came to Sumter County from Twiggs County about 1831. He first built a log house on the Old Stage Road between Americus and Oglethorpe, about two miles southeast of the present

Hodges Plantation home. The well-kept and still used Hodges family cemetery is near the site of the log home.

When the Civil War broke out, Robert James Hodges was 46 years old and married to Matilda Caroline Hill, his second wife. His first wife, Rebecca Davenport Hodges had died in 1852. He was the father of three daughters by his first wife—Anna, 20, Bell, 19, Henrietta Caroline, 18, and four boys by his second wife—Robert James Hodges, Jr., 7, David Hill, 5, Willis Spencer, 4, and Bonton Hill, the baby. (Three more children were to be born to the couple, Rodolph in 1863, Algernon Freneau, and Matilda, after the War.) He was a respected landowner—the Hodges Plantation then contained 3000 acres—and a local office holder, being a judge of the inferior court of Sumter County. This was an appointive position usually conferred upon the best educated man in the community, for any degree of formal education was rare in those days. The duties of the inferior court included building and seeing to the upkeep of county roads with volunteered slave labor, taking care of the needs of the poor, seeing to the hiring of teachers and the upkeep of schools, keeping law and order, and trying small cases not important enough for a higher court. Inferior court judges were also authorized to perform marriages. It was an unpaid and probably a thankless job.

It was natural that the Confederate committee in charge of selecting a site for a war prison should, when contemplating the Andersonville area, turn to Judge Hodges for the facts in matters concerning whether the area near Andersonville was suitable for such a prison. According to Hodges family history, Judge Hodges declared the area previously free of fever and other maladies and he thought a good supply of clear water could be had in the vicinity.

It was also natural that Judge Hodges become acquainted with members of the Andersonville Prison Confederate commander's staff and invite members of that staff to his home. Records show that Robert James Hodges served as chaplain for the Confederate forces stationed at Andersonville. Besides running his 3000-acre plantation, Judge Hodges was in demand as a preacher for area churches, at least one of which he was instrumental in building—century old Salem Methodist, still operating in the nearby New Era Community. According to an old family story, Judge Hodges never accepted any pay for his preaching and always said, "If the congregation can work all week and then come and sit in church on Sunday, the least I can do is preach without pay."

Judge Hodges built his permanent home in a stand of oak trees near the Stage Road which ran between Americus and Oglethorpe.

Hodges Plantation home as it looks today.

Today, that part of the Stage Road has disappeared, but the oaks, now more than one hundred feet high and some with big gnarled wisteria vines growing up their entire height—a sight to behold when in bloom—still guard the house.

The original part of the present-day house consisted of nine rooms —five downstairs and four upstairs. The front part of the house was high-ceilinged and the rear low ceilinged. Square columns from the ground level piazza to the second-story roof gave a certain elegance to the front entrance.

The ground floor was bisected by a wide high-ceilinged hall, designed to provide natural air-conditioning, with a large parlor on either side of the hall. The kitchen, set off a little way from the east side of the house because of the fire hazard and heat from open hearth cooking, was connected to the house by a runway.

Today, a potpourri of keepsakes of three generations of the Hodges family plus heirlooms from the families of their wives are in evidence throughout the house. A collection of approximately a hundred antique dolls, some dating back to the early 1800's, lend interest to the front parlors. This collection has been a hobby for many years of Mrs. R. J. (Fannie) Hodges, the present owner. Dominating the dining room behind the east parlor is a long mahogany dining table which seats twelve and a cherry sideboard which Matilda Caroline Hill, Robert James Hodges' second wife, brought to the house at the time of her marriage in 1853.

The high-ceilinged parlors have been the scene of eight weddings— the daughters of each generation being married at home. Henrietta Caroline Hodges was married to William R. Methvin in 1863; Belle Hodges and Robert Alexander Brown were married in October 1866, and Albeanna Hodges and John Shiver one month later in November 1866.

The two daughters of Algernon F. Hodges, Rebecca and Ruth, were also married at home, Rebecca to Penn Scott in 1915 and Ruth to Roger A. Jennings in 1920.

Frances and Ruth Hodges, daughters of Robert James Hodges III and Fannie Little Hodges, were more recent brides. Frances was married to Collins Sullivan in 1953 and Ruth to Frederick Frick in 1971.

Part of what was formerly the back porch has been made into a family room by the present owners, using original shutters which had been stored in an outbuilding, across one wall. The original hand hewn door frame lends charm to this room as do the hand blown panes of glass on either side of the back door to the wide hall. On the wall is the powder horn and 1830 rifle used by Robert James Hodges when he went as a young man to Florida to help fight in an Indian uprising. Among the framed mementoes on the wall is a collection of Indian arrowheads found on the plantation and an eight hundred and twenty-seven dollar slave bill-of-sale made out to William Stinson, great-great-grandfather of Mrs. Fannie Hodges, for "two new Negroes to use and behoff forever" and dated "in the twenty-seventh year of the independence of the United States of America."

Judge Hodges' children and grandchildren were taught at home by tutors who lived in the home. One of the small rear upstairs rooms was furnished as a schoolroom with desks and a blackboard. Miss Linda Mathis, who later taught for more than 35 years in the Americus public schools, was in 1907 the last tutor in the home. "Miss Linda" taught the five children of Judge Hodges' son, Algernon F. Hodges— Ruth, Rebecca, John, Robert, and Algernon, Jr. She says her father drove her out from Americus in a horse-and-buggy each Sunday evening and she stayed during the week with the Hodges family, but

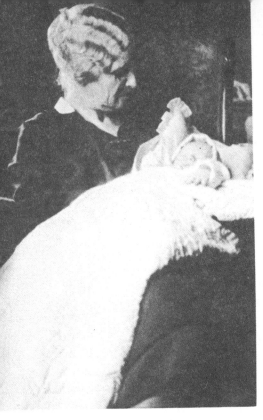

*Mrs. Algernon F. Hodges,
neé Emma Battle, holding
her grandson, Roger A.
Jennings Jr. in 1928.*

*The present Mrs. Robert
Hodges with one of her
many antique dolls.*

spent weekends at home in Americus. "I was only about nineteen when I taught the Hodges children," she recalls. "We kept regular school hours from about 8 a.m. until 3 p.m. Sometimes in the afternoons after school, I'd accompany the children on jaunts over the farm. We'd ride mules to the cane patch or to the creek. One night I went 'possum hunting with them and they made me tote the 'possums in a sack."

A huge iron washpot, a relic of the days of Judge Hodges when it was used not only to boil clothes but to render lard at hog killing time, is still on the premises and in good condition. A family story told by Grandmother Hodges, the Judge's second wife, is recalled with humor by Mrs. Fannie Hodges: "In the eighteen hundreds, the washpot sat in the backyard where it was visible from the Old Stage Road. After the War, carpetbaggers from the North traveled the South to see the conquered land. They usually traveled the stage roads, sometimes on foot. One of these carpetbaggers appeared on the road on foot and stood a long time looking into the yard. Finally, he asked if he might get in that big pot. 'Why in the world do you want to get in our washpot?' he was asked. 'When I go home, I want to tell my friends up North that I saw a washpot so big that I could get my whole self in it,' he declared. He was a small man and managed to get in, wriggle around and curl himself up inside the pot—but he was not so successful in getting out and found himself stuck. Grandmother Hodges is reported to have said afterwards that she was tempted to leave that meddlesome Yankee in the pot and start a fire under him, but she instructed some of the Negroes to pull him out."

Many reminders of the farming enterprises of Judge Hodges are still in evidence in the area. To the west of the house stands the century-old log corn crib with cedar shake roof which was built by Judge Hodges before the Civil War. Between the house and the town of Andersonville, where Viney Branch runs into Sweet Water Creek, the Judge dug a canal and built a grist mill. During the occupation of Andersonville Prison, this mill was used to grind cornmeal for the use of both the prisoners and the guards. Although the old mill was abandoned about 1915, the site remained popular for Sunday school and public school picnics well into the twentieth century. Miss Nettie Mae Peek, life-long resident of the area, remembers her Andersonville High School graduating class picnicking there in 1925.

One field on the Hodges Plantation is called "vineyard cut" because it is where Judge Hodges planted eight acres of scuppernongs, both black and white varieties, to supply the family with wine. The vines thrived and have supplied three generations of the family with scuppernongs.

John Hodges, Algernon F. Hodges, Jr., "Bob Tail Steer" and Robert J. Hodges on Hodges Plantation about 1900.

Last tutor for Hodges children was Miss Linda Mathis pictured in front of Hodges home in 1907.

Algernon F. Hodges was elected to the Georgia Legislature September 12, 1928.

Robert James Hodges III, most recent master of the Hodges Plantation, was an avid hunter and fisherman.

A hill on the plantation near the house contains high-grade clay. When Judge Hodges was building the house, clay from that site was used by slaves to make brick for the chimneys and pillars. About thirty years ago, the handmade brick in the pillars were replaced, but those in the dining room fireplace remain in good condition.

Algernon F. Hodges, youngest child of Judge Hodges, took over the management of the plantation after the death of his father in 1883. He was active in public life, serving as a Sumter County commissioner and in 1929 he was elected to the Georgia Legislature. His wife, Emma Battle Hodges, was active in the United Daughters of the Confederacy and in the Primitive Baptist Church of Andersonville. When the yearly district Primitive Baptist Association meeting was held in Andersonville, she opened her home to delegates, sometimes having as many as 30 extra people staying at the house. (Where needed, pallets were arranged on the floor for sleeping accommodations.) Her oldest son, John Randolph Hodges, weary of the visitors, is said to have declared that when he had a home of his own, no one would ever again get him to give up his bed to a church delegate.

Emma Battle Hodges, who had trouble with her eyesight after a childhood bout with measles, received a further setback to her sight as a matron of fifty when ether accidently got into her eyes when she was undergoing an operation. Her poor eyesight made it impossible for her to do much reading, but she was a person who liked to keep up with current events and enjoyed literature. She made it a house rule that any member of the family who read anything in her presence, must read it aloud. "I'm interested in everything," she'd say. "I don't care what it is, read aloud. You can read orally as well as silently." She also prevailed upon a blind neighbor who had attended a school for the blind to teach her to read Braille. In her later years, she became interested in securing an REA line to the rural Andersonville area. She circulated petitions, wrote to her congressman, and even wrote to President Franklin D. Roosevelt. Her campaign was finally successful and the REA power lines came to the Hodges and neighboring farms in 1937, but Emma Battle Hodges had died a few months before the power was turned on.

Algernon and Emma's two oldest sons, John Randolph Hodges and Robert James Hodges III, farmed with their father until his death in 1934 and then continued farming on their own. John built a house for himself and his wife, Mattie Horne Hodges, and their five children on the Old Stage Road not far from where the first Robert James Hodges built his log house. Robert and his wife, Fannie Little Hodges, and their four children continued to live in the homeplace.

Robert James Hodges III, the most recent master of the plantation, had attended the University of Georgia one year, Georgia Tech one year, and graduated from Kentucky's Bolling Green Business School and served in an artillery unit in World War I before settling down to farming. He was an outdoorsman who loved hunting and fishing and for relaxation roamed the woods and fields of his own place and those of his neighbors looking for deer, duck, quail, dove, rabbit, and 'possum. His children claimed that he had a horse and dog so well trained that when he signaled, the horse froze and the dog pointed. His favorite hunting companion was Charles Crisp, Sr., president of the Bank of Commerce in Americus. For almost five decades, the two men never missed hunting together in Sumter County on the opening day of the duck season and were frequent companions during dove and quail seasons.

The two sons of Robert and Fannie Hodges have taken up other pursuits—Robert James Hodges IV undertook a career in the United States Air Force from which he recently retired as a Lieutenant Colonel and Forrester Little Hodges now runs his own furniture manufacturing company in Fayetteville, Georgia. Today, the homeplace, now about a thousand acres, is rented out to Leon and Howard Holloway who raise grain, cattle, and pecans, but Warren Freneau Hodges, the son of John Randolph and Mattie Hodges, lives on and operates the 500 acres his father once managed.

10

Andersonville
Mining Activities

THE TOWN OF ANDERSONVILLE, during the time of the prison, included a post office, a depot, a blacksmith shop and stable, a couple of general stores, two saloons, a school, a Methodist church, and about a dozen houses. (Ben Dykes, who owned the land on which the prison was built, was both depot agent and postmaster.) Two miles south of town at Gardner Spring was Mt. Olive Baptist Church. On Sweetwater Creek, south of town was Robert James Hodges' grist mill. Also in the area was a two-story mill owned by Ben Dykes. Farmlands surrounding the town were owned by Robert James Hodges, Ben Dykes, Bennet Easterlin, John Comer Peek, Levi Matison Holloway, and Josh Cunningham.

Until the establishment of the prison, the area was entirely dependent on agriculture, and, after the close of the prison, the town continued economically dependent on agriculture. The town changed very little over the years, until 1968 when the mining of kaolin, bauxitic kaolin, and bauxite was undertaken in a big way by Mulcoa, Mullite Company of America which has turned 2000 acres of scrub oak wilderness into a massive mining and refining operation and now ship more than 2000 tons of refined ore from Andersonville each week.

The potential for a lucrative mining industry had been present in the Andersonville area long before the town was established. Reference was made at the Wirz trial to the presence of clay and iron in the prison soil. Robert Kellogg, prisoner, testified, "The slope rising from Stockade Branch to the north was sand with large admixtures of clay and sand as well as the oxide of iron, which forms in its various combinations a cement to the sand, favored tunneling."

Sporadic activities in mining bauxite and kaolin were made in the early 1900's. In 1932, American Cyanimid Company started mining and shipping bauxite from the area, and in 1971 opened calcining facilities in neighboring Macon County. In 1968, through the efforts of Andersonville's mayor, Lewis Easterlin, Mullitte Company came to Andersonville.

"The Andersonville area of Sumter County contains probably

Mulcoa, Mullite Company of America has turned 2000 acres of scrub oak wilderness into a massive mining and refining operation.

80

Lewis Easterlin
long time mayor of Andersonville.

the richest deposits of kaolin, bauxitic kaolin, and bauxite in this country and quite probably the richest deposits in the entire world," claims George R. Eusner, president of Andersonville's Mullite Company which is mining the ore, processing it, and shipping it to many sections of the United States, Germany, Japan, and other parts of the world.

Mr. Eusner, who formerly headed the refractory and mineral technology of United States Steel, Inc., and Lewis Easterlin, whose family once owned much of the kaolin and bauxite-rich land and whose uncle handmined kaolin with the help of a mule team and a dozen fieldhands in the early 1900's, started Mullite Company in 1968. Later, Mullite became a subsidiary of Combustion Engineering, Inc., but it now operates as an independent plant with Mr. Eusner as president and Mr. Easterlin as vice-president. In its first year the company shipped 150 tons a week.

"That seemed like a great deal to me," says Lewis Easterlin. "My uncle used to ship two boxcars a year—mostly to the city of Columbus to use in purifying the city water supply. Our first year's output of 150 tons a week proved to be 'a drop in the bucket.' In less than two years we doubled our output to 300 tons a week and now with the addition of new kilns and expansion of our plant floor to one-half million square feet, we have more than doubled that record to 2000 tons of finished product a week."

The calcined bauxite ore is in great demand and is used primarily as refractory materials for the steel industry, such as fire brick for

81

lining blast furnaces, blast furnace stoves, open hearth furnaces, electric furnaces, and in the nosecones of space ships. Mr. Eusner estimates that almost two million tons of this type of material is used annually in the United States.

The raw materials of kaolin, bauxitic kaolin, and bauxite are mined from open pits with huge crawler-type tractors and dumped in mountain-sized stockpiles from which they are moved by truck to the plant.

The mining process at Mullite goes on 365 days a year, twenty-four hours a day, because of the great demand for the refined product and because the huge cylinder-shaped kilns, which are heated to 3000 degrees Farhenheit, would take too long to cool and reheat if shut down at night.

After being dried and cleaned, the raw material is placed in an auger machine which extrudes it under 28 inches of vacuum in long cylinders. From there it is fed into the rotary kilns. After being cooled, the product is moved to crushers and over screens for later loading into railroad cars. When all equipment is functioning properly, the plant can be run from an ultra-modern room resembling a moon-shot control tower at Cape Kennedy.

Although the plant is completely automated, seventy-five men are employed in the mining and refining operation. The miners and plant workers are paid on an hourly basis with the payroll usually exceeding $15,000 a week.

The problem of air pollution, which appeared at the beginning of the mining operation in the form of white dust, has been, at the expense of more than a million dollars to the company, almost eliminated. Huge water reservoirs on top of the buildings and a lake behind the plant, are maintained to catch and filter the dust out of the air.

Through the foresight of long-time Mayor Easterlin (he's served in that capacity for almost 20 years) the town of Andersonville obtained natural gas service about the time that Mullite settled in the area. The Andersonville Natural Gas Commission sells gas to town residents and businesses. Mullite, its largest single customer, uses over 100,000 cubit feet of natural gas every twenty-four hours. The plant's monthly bill runs over $60,000.

Mayor Easterlin says, "Townspeople had been asking me for many years to try to obtain an industry for Andersonville in order to bring an economic lift to the town and to offer job opportunities to our young people. Mullite is the perfect industry for us. Our natural resources, tons and tons of kaolin and bauxite, have been here under the ground for millions of years. Now at last, through the knowledge and technical know-how of George Eusner, we are able to turn these natural resources into products much needed in this technological age."

Officials of American Cyanimid Company in front of calcining plant.

11

The Mystery of Andersonville
Methodist Church

ANDERSONVILLE METHODIST CHURCH has been in existence for more than a century ministering to the spiritual needs of its tiny congregaticn. Two events, one hundred years apart, stand out in the history of the church—the commandeering of the original church building as living quarters for members of the Andersonville Prison stockade commander's staff and the substantial legacy left to the church by a mysterious benefactor.

In 1965, the total membership of the church was 48. That year, a letter from a New Jersey lawyer informed the members that the church had been left the income from an estate valued at more than $178,000. The church treasurer, Margaret Holloway, a young farm housewife, was the startled recipient of this letter which stated that the Andersonville Methodist Church was the chief beneficiary of the estate of Robert B. Brown who died in Washington, New Jersey.

By nightfall, everybody in Andersonville—the population then was 281—had heard the news, and the church officials were gathered for a meeting. "That means most of the 25 active members were present," laughs Margaret Holloway. "In a church our size, if you are active at all, you are either a steward, an officer, the Sunday School superintendent, on the board of directors—or something."

The first thing to come out of that called meeting was that nobody had ever heard of Robert B. Brown.

In a second letter from Washington, New Jersey were the facts that Robert B. Brown died at the age of 90, that in his 80th year he approached an attorney on the subject of his will. He told the lawyer that he had no family, no church affiliation, no special interest in any charitable organization, and no close friends. He related that once several years back, he was traveling in Georgia and feeling unusually alone. He happened to hear a church bell ringing. On impulse, he decided to attend church services. He entered the Andersonville Methodist Church, a stranger, and was given a warm welcome. He had never forgotten the genuine kindness of the people of that church.

"I might as well leave what I have to that little church," he told his lawyer. "At least they are not hypocrites."

84

Church members subsequently learned that Robert B. Brown died on February 20, 1965. His will was drawn up in 1955. Members figure that his visit to Andersonville Methodist Church could have been anywhere from fifteen to twenty-five years before his death. Robert B. Brown still remains a mystery. All anyone knows is that he lived alone in a furnished room, owned little else besides his investments, a television set, and his clothes. According to his New Jersey attorney, "Mr. Brown was an extremely thrifty man who kept to himself, but when he did contact the outside world, he appeared to me to have an engaging personality, a lively wit, and a rather philosophical outlook on the world." At the bottom of the page of notes he prepared about his will, he wrote, *Sic transit gloria mundi.*

The lawyer's letter arrived in Andersonville in 1965 and people have been searching their memories ever since—but no one can say for sure that he remembers Robert B. Brown.

What has this little church done with its windfall? Has the money changed the personalities of the members? Has it changed life in Andersonville?

"Well, our church never needed a lawyer before," said Alex M. Rouse, chairman of the Official Board, "but we immediately retained the services of an Americus attorney and we're glad we did. Immediately after an Associated Press story on our unusual bequest was released to the newspapers, we were the recipients of a good deal of mail from all parts of the nation. A man from Texas, who claimed kinship with Robert B. Brown, demanded $25,000 at once—or he would take the matter to court. Our lawyer informed him that we did not have $25,000 and that all we would ever receive at one time would be $5000, the approximate yearly income from the estate. We never heard from the Texan again, but there were others claiming a share of the money, or suggesting ways to spend it. Our lawyer dealt successfully with all of them."

Most of the membership of the church comes from eight families in Andersonville—the Holloways, the Rouses, the Johnsons, Hobbs, Rays, Bells, Davises, and Kratzes. Before Mr. Brown's generous gift, these eight families had pretty much carried the financial needs of the church themselves and dipped deep into their pockets to do it—as had generations of their families before them.

In 1947, a new $10,000 structure was built to replace the old building which was totally demolished in a freak cyclone, the second time a storm had destroyed Andersonville's Methodist Church. The debt brought on by the 1947 building program had been paid off in full before Mr. Brown's bequest. Also, prior to this event, the members had installed and fully paid for an organ and an air conditioner.

Andersonville Methodist Church

Margaret Holloway was first to hear of mystery man's bequest.

Today, the active members still meet the needs of the church budget. The income from Mr. Brown's bequest goes into a "special fund" and is used for special needs.

Mr. Brown's money has helped two deserving young people get the college education they were struggling to achieve themselves. One was a ministerial student at Emory. The other, a local girl who grew up a member of the Andersonville Methodist Church, was working her way through the University of Georgia waiting on tables in the cafeteria and helping in the University library, when the church stepped in and paid off a debt she had incurred in order to pay her tuition.

The church's "special fund" has given a financial helping hand to several local senior citizens in need, and to a 12-year-old boy who broke his neck in a dive into a shallow farm pond and spent several months in the Columbus Medical Center. It helped a small south Georgia church which was experiencing financial troubles, and it financed a new $20,000 brick parsonage, a car for the preacher, and made possible a generous donation to the Methodist Dooly Campground program, which benefits hundreds of young people from all parts of south Georgia.

"Miss Hattie" Holloway, oldest member of the church and a student of the Bible, compares Mr. Brown's unusual gift and the chain of events that has followed to the Parable of the Mustard Seed. "Just look at the fruit borne by the tiny seed of kindness sown long ago," she marvels.

12

Jimmy Lawrence and Pennington Saint James Church

ONE BLOCK WEST from the center of the town of Andersonville stands the quaint little architectural gem, Pennington St. James Church. The tiny log church, originally situated deep in the Georgia woods 2½ miles southeast of Andersonville on Highway 195, was moved in 1975 to its present site and restored by the Andersonville Guild.

Pennington Saint James, the little church in the woods, was started by James Bolan Lawrence, the sort of Protestant minister who, had he lived a century earlier, would have been compelled to follow the Catholic priest, Father Peter Whelan, into Andersonville Prison and minister spiritually to the prisoners. However, Dr. Lawrence was born thirteen years after the prison was closed. Instead of ministering to Andersonville prisoners, he made it his mission in life to offer a helping hand to the descendents of Confederates in Sumter County and especially in the Andersonville area.

Dr. Lawrence, 40 years rector of Calvary Episcopal Church of Americus, built Pennington Saint James as a mission church. Constructed in 1927 out of native fieldstone and hand hewn cypress logs according to a design of Cramm and Ferguson, nationally-known Boston architects who designed the Cathedral of St. John the Divine in New York City, the church originally stood on property deeded at that time to the Episcopal diocese of Georgia by W. E., A. E., and W. M. Pennington who lived nearby and whose families all became members of Pennington Saint James. The building was erected through the financial cooperation of all denominations in Americus where Dr. Lawrence was well known and much loved and through the physical efforts of Episcopalians of the community with Dr. Lawrence himself, a tall muscular bachelor, doing a good part of the actual labor.

From 1927 until a year after Dr. Lawrence's death in 1947, there was never a Sunday, no matter how ill the weather, without a service being held in the beauty and serenity of the little church in the woods. Services were held on all holy days of the year and communion was served communicants there once a month. Easter sunrise services were attended by many non-Episcopalians from Americus and the surround-

Dr. James Bolan Lawrence

ing area. Eleven marriages were performed there and about fifteen former members of the church are buried there.

Mrs. Marlie Dunaway of Americus, who played the old-fashioned pump organ at Pennington Saint James every Sunday for more than 20 years, says, "Dr. Lawrence conducted services at Calvary Episcopal Church in Americus each Sunday morning. After Sunday dinner, he would start out from Americus in the company of a few members of the Calvary Church for the 10-mile trip to Andersonville. His large old car would stop along the way at isolated farms to pick up children for the afternoon Sunday school class at Pennington.

"These children and their families were his particular concern," she states. "Many were poor and he clothed them. Friends from New York City sent boxes of clothing periodically. He encouraged the young people to further their education and helped several toward admittance to college with financial backing. Each Christmas season a Christmas tree party was held at Pennington Saint James with fine presents for everyone. He persuaded a friend who owned a marble mining company in north Georgia to donate a truckload of slabs of marble suitable for tombstones and arranged for the church to provide free properly inscribed tombstones for members buried in the churchyard."

Pennington St. James Episcopal Church as it appeared in 1930.

Annually on Saint James Day, July 25, Pennington Community was host at an old-fashioned outdoor barbecue for guests and members of the church. The barbecue, usually prepared by Ernest Pantone, friend of the church, was free and attracted large crowds.

Dr. Lawrence, a sincerely dedicated man of God, was unique in that area as to the formal education he had acquired in preparation for the ministry and in his charisma with all types of people with various religious backgrounds. Before going into the ministry, he received a Bachelor of Arts and a Master of Arts degree from the University of Georgia, a Bachelor of Divinity from General Theological Seminary in New York City, and he had taught Greek at the University of Georgia which in 1928 conferred the degree of Doctor of Divinity upon him. He was a friend of all he met, rich or poor, black or white— but the poor and unfortunate were his particular care. He was forever sending habitual drunks to the hospital or to one of the Americus hotels to be cared for at his expense. His Negro friends were numbered by the thousands. When "Uncle John," the Negro sextant of Calvary Church, died, Dr. Lawrence preached the funeral service at Uncle John's Negro church. When old Mr. Louis Rosenberg, an Americus Jewish merchant, celebrated his 80th birthday, Dr. Lawrence had a birthday party for him, inviting many prominent business people of the town. Dr. Lawrence, who read Hebrew and Greek, translated the Episcopal Birthday Prayer into Hebrew and read it at the party—which so touched old Mr. Rosenberg that tears ran down his face. These and many other thoughtful acts endeared Dr. Lawrence to the people of Americus and Sumter County, who always affectionately called him, "Brother Lawrence."

On Saturday, June 21, 1913, Americus was aroused over the shooting of Chief of Police W. C. Barrow by a Negro man, Will Redding. An hour after the shooting, an angry mob broke into the Sumter County jail bent on lynching Redding. Brother Lawrence, along with another Americus minister, stood between the Negro and the mob and pled for the lynching party to disperse and that the accused be allowed to stand trial. Brother Lawrence considered it one of the greatest failures of his life that he and his colleague were not successful in stopping the lynching. The next day, Sunday, he put his feelings about the lynching into an impassioned sermon condemning the action of the crowd.

Dr. Lawrence served several other little country congregations near Americus, and he spent one month each summer as rector of St. Mary's Church at 521 West 126th Street, New York City—but he had a special feeling for Pennington and planned to build a home there upon his retirement. Cramm and Ferguson, architectural firm in which he had personal friends, drew up plans for his retirement home. The foundation had been laid at the time of Brother Lawrence's death and is still standing today.

During his month each summer as rector of St. Mary's in the Harlem section of New York City, Brother Lawrence always designated one Sunday as "Georgia Day" when Georgians in the Manhattan area were invited to a Georgia style dinner-on-the-grounds in the small church yard in the heart of Manhattan. Such was Brother Lawrence's magnetism that prominent former Americus citizens such as Gertrude Davenport, designer of the Wraparong and other terrycloth originals which led to the nationally-known Tog Shop mail order business, annually found themselves enjoying a family style Georgia get-together with black citizens of Harlem.

It is a sad commentary on our times that the little Pennington St. James Church, Brother Lawrence's dream, which stood proudly and serenely on its former site for more than 50 years, was in the late 1960's ransacked by vandals. Vandals carried off piece by piece, the stained glass windows, the altar rail, the heavy pine doors, and the 300 books carefully selected by Brother Lawrence for a free lending library for that remote community.

Among the gravestones at the former site are two huge rocks landscaped with flowers and shrubbery. The largest marks the last resting place of Brother Lawrence and bears this inscription:

JAMES BOLAN LAWRENCE D.D.
BORN 1878
DIED 1947

Brother Lawrence had moved both rocks in a pickup truck from the other side of Sumter County to their present site for the beautification of the church yard. A friend snapped a picture of him sitting on the rock underneath which it was his desire to be buried. He wrote the following poem on the back of the snapshot:

> To-day I sit and rest upon my Rock;
> Someday my Rock will lie and rest on me.
>
> My Rock and I are hewn from one same block.
> Today I sit and rest upon my Rock.
>
> O Rock of Ages, cross nor nail nor mock
> May part us—Thee in me and me in Thee.
>
> To-day I sit and rest upon my Rock;
> Someday my Rock will lie and rest on me.

BIBLIOGRAPHY

Ashe, Sarah W. *The Trial and Death of Henry Wirz.* Raleigh: E. M. Uzzell and Conmpany, 1908.

Bearss, Edwin C. *Andersonville National Historic Site.* Washington, D. C.: U. S. Department of the Interior, Office of History and Historic Architecture, Eastern Service Center, July 31, 1970.

Chipman, N. P. *The Tragedy of Andersonville.* San Francisco: The Blair-Murdock Company, 1911.

Futch, Ovid L. *History of Andersonville Prison.* Gainesville: University of Florida Press, 1968.

"Hodges, A. F." Biographical Information for the Georgia Department of Archives and History, 1928.

Kerr, Dr. W. J. W. "Sad Ending of a Wedding Trip." *Confederate Veteran,* XXIII, 7 (July, 1915) p. 318.

"Lynching Was Characterized by Savagery." *The Americus Times Recorder,* June 24, 1913.

Maile, John L. *Prison Life In Andersonville.* Los Angeles: Press of West Coast Magazine, 1912.

Minutes of the Fourteenth Annual Convention of the Georgia Division United Daughters of the Confederacy, Savannah, Georgia, October 1908.

Minutes of the Fifteenth Annual Convention of the Georgia Division United Daughters of the Confederacy, West Point, Georgia, November 1909.

Pennsylvania at Andersonville, Georgia, Ceremonies at the Dedication of the Memorial, 1905.

Peterson, William J. "Benjamin F. Gue." *The Palimpsest,* XLII (June 1961), pp. 209-210.

Ransom, John L. *Andersonville Diary, Escape and List of the Dead.* published by the author, Auburn, N. Y. 1881.

Rutherford, Mildred Lewis. "The Truth About Henry Wirz," *Historical Essay Contest.* Athens, Georgia: Georgia Division UDC, 1921.

"Shaft to Wirz," *Americus Weekly Times-Recorder,* Thursday, May 13, 1909.

Sheppard, Peggy "Andersonville's Mysterious Benefactor," *Georgia Magazine* XIV, 2 (August-September 1970), p. 14.

Sibley, Celestine, "Lancaster's Appeal Defeats Wirz Statue," *Atlanta Constitution,* February 20, 1958.

Spencer, Ambrose. *A Narrative of Andersonville.* New York: Harper and Brothers, 1866.

Stevenson, R. Randolph. *The Southern Side, Or, Andersonville Prison.* Baltimore: Turnbull Brothers, 1876.

Sumter County Ordinary, Marriage Licenses, Book 4, pp. 116, 145, 248, 288.

Sumter County Ordinary, Marriage Licenses, Book 5, p. 185

Trial Of Henry Wirz, House Executive Documents, 40th Congress, 2nd Session, Series 1331, Robert Kellogg's Testimony. p. 64.

U. S. Bureau of Refugees, Freedman, and Abandoned Lands, Education Division, microfilm at the Department of Archives and History, Atlanta, Georgia.

SUPPLEMENTARY SOURCES

Helpful information and references came from interviews with the following people from Andersonville: Lewis Easterlin, George Eusner, Paul Gordon, Mrs. John Hodges, Mrs. Robert Hodges, Mrs. Leon Holloway, Mrs. Clara Belle Peek Johnson, Miss Nettie Mae Peek, and Mrs. Lorenza Cotton and the following residents of Americus: Lloyd Caswell, Lucius McCleskey, Mrs. Marlie Dunaway, Miss Josephine Easterlin, Miss Linda Mathis, Mrs. Janet Merritt.

About the Author

The author of this collection of twelve stories concerning Andersonville—the old prison, the trial of Captain Henry Wirz, the report of Clara Barton, the agonizing experiences of many who had differing views concerning the whole sad chapter of American history—includes in this volume sketches never before presented of the people and places of the area, right down to the present year of 1973.

This book *is* Andersonville, Georgia, USA—1973.

A glance at the bibliography should give the reader confidence in the scope of her research.

Who better than Peggy Arbuckle Sheppard could present a more objective view?

Born in Yonkers, New York, she spent summers at Brewster, on Cape Cod in Massachusetts until she met Fred Shipp Sheppard of Americus, Georgia in 1945 and came with him to Sumter County in 1946 as his bride.

Her husband, a native of Americus, was at the time of their meeting a Lieutenant Commander in the U. S. Maritime Service and Skipper of the Victory Ship *Aiken Victory* which was in and out of New York harbor.

Leaving the service and returning to Americus they bought 850 acres of farm land in Sumter County, later naming it *Aching Acres,* as a double play on the name of his ship and their experience in farming.

Peggy, having completed three years of study at Syracuse University in New York, was soon drafted into the Sumter County school system as a teacher in a three-room rural school. She continued her education at Georgia State College for Women at Milledgeville, from which she received her degree. In 1968, after twenty-two years of successful teaching she retired. Through sale, their acreage has been reduced to about 150 acres so that now she can devote more time to what she has long wanted to do—writing. She, her husband and their son, Lee, continue to live at *Aching Acres* which is only about fifteen miles from Andersonville, about which she has written in this volume.

She sold her first article to *GEORGIA Magazine* in 1959 and since then has continued as a regular contributor. She is now Culinary Editor of this state-oriented magazine. In the meantime she has written for many other publications, including: *Farm Journal,* published in

Philadelphia; *Successful Farming* of Des Moines, Iowa; the Columbus, Georgia *Ledger-Enquirer Sunday Magazine,* and *The Atlanta Journal-Constitution Sunday Magazine* as well as *Guideposts, Children's Friend* and many other educational journals.

Peggy Sheppard is one of those rare people in this world—she is dependable—she sees things as they are—and she tells it as it is!

We wholeheartedly recommend this book to readers everywhere.

DECATUR, GEORGIA
MAY 6, 1973
Ann E. Lewis
Editor and Publisher, *Georgia Magazine*

Providence Springs—Photo Courtesy National Park Service